SUNSET
TO
SUNRISE

Night Flight Techniques

SUNSET
TO
SUNRISE
Night Flight Techniques

DAVID ROBSON

A Focus Series Book
Aviation Supplies & Academics, Inc.
Newcastle, Washington

Sunset to Sunrise: Night Flight Techniques
by David P. Robson

Aviation Supplies & Academics, Inc.
7005 132nd Place SE
Newcastle, Washington 98059-3153
www.asa2fly.com

Published 2004 by Aviation Supplies & Academics, Inc.

Acknowledgments
Photographs: Aviation Theory Centre
Graphics: Rob Loriente
Layout and index: Catherine Jeffreys

Printed in Canada

ISBN 1-56027-542-1

ASA-NIGHT

Contents

Chapter 3

Part 2: Night Flight Rules and Requirements

Chapter 6
Night Flight Technique 107

Chapter 7
Abnormal Operations at Night 131

Author/Editor

David Robson

David Robson is a career aviator having been nurtured on balsa wood, dope (the legal kind), and tissue paper. He made his first solo flight shortly after his seventeenth birthday, having made his first parachute jump just after his sixteenth. His first job was as a junior draftsman (they weren't persons in those days) at the Commonwealth Aircraft Corporation in Melbourne, Australia. At that time he was also learning to fly in Chipmunks with the Royal Victorian Aero Club. He joined the Royal Australian Air Force in 1965 and served for twenty-one years as a fighter pilot and test pilot. He flew over 1,000 hours on Mirages and 500 on Sabres. He completed the Empire Test Pilots' course at Boscombe Down in 1972, flying everything from gliders to Lightnings and Argosies. He completed a tour in Vietnam as a forward air controller in sup-

port of the First Australian Task Force. He was a member of the Mirage formation aerobatic team, the Deltas, which celebrated the RAAF's 50th anniversary.

After retiring from the Air Force, David became a civilian instructor and lecturer and spent over ten years with the Australian Aviation College. During 1986-88, he was the editor of the *Aviation Safety Digest* (the "Crash Comic") which won the Flight Safety Foundation's international award. He was awarded the Australian Aviation Safety Foundation's Certificate of Air Safety in 1997 and the Award for Excellence in training in 2001. He continues to fly at Morrabbin, Ballarat, and Temora.

Editorial Team

Jackie Spanitz

Jackie earned a B.S. in Aviation Technology and Operations from Western Michigan University and earned a M.S. from Embry-Riddle Aeronautical University. As Curriculum Director for ASA, Jackie oversees new and existing product development, ranging from textbooks and flight computers to computer-based tutorials, and integration of these products into curricula. She also conducts aviation research as well as product development and project management. She holds Flight and Ground Instructor Certificates. Jackie is the author of *Guide to the Biennial Flight Review* and the technical editor for ASA's Test Prep Series.

Melanie Waddell

Melanie began flying in 1994 and was awarded a Bachelor of Technology in aviation studies in 1997 from Swinburne University, Melbourne, Australia. She currently holds an ATPL, with multi-engine and command instrument ratings, and is a grade-one flight instructor at Essendon. To broaden her aeronautical knowledge and experience, she instructed the Air Training Corps and was appointed acting flight commander of 5 Flight in the Victorian Squadron. She has also worked for Airshows Downunder. She continues to pursue a challenging career in aviation. Melanie and her husband, Darren, were recently married in a DC-3!

Juliet Dyer

Juliet began flying training at the age of 15 in Melbourne, Australia. She successfully studied for a Bachelor of Science (Aviation) degree at Newcastle University and after gaining a commercial pilot's license was employed as a scenic pilot conducting flights along the beautiful South Coast of New South Wales. She returned to Melbourne to complete her tertiary studies at Swinburne University, concentrating on aviation business management, at the same time completing a Flight Instructor's rating at Moorabbin.

Introduction

Night flight is magnificent. It is smooth, uncluttered, and easy, provided you learn the correct technique and you fly regularly. Night flying technique is the same as day flight, except you probably will not have a visual horizon. There is, therefore, only one way to fly at night: by the instruments. However, there are two ways of navigating (visually and by NAVAIDs) and two sets of rules and procedures (IFR and VFR). Each has its own pros and cons.

Why Fly at Night, Especially in a Single-Engine Airplane?

Some of the aspects that can make night flight such a pleasant experience include smooth conditions, good visibility, reduced wind, traffic, talking, and thermal activity, wonderful sunsets (and sunrises if you are an early riser), and beautiful patterns of stars and lights. Moreover, there are the added advantages of increased aircraft utilization, better takeoff and climb performance, better visibility (greater distances), fewer birds (although you may encounter bats and other animal activity), easier and faster service at FBOs, and more readily available aircraft rentals. But night flight has its potential hazards—you may not see an embedded thunderstorm inside a stratus cloud, the ADF needle can give false indications at night, and there are few lights and many illusions over sea, desert, and mountains. Like all forms of flight, night flight should be approached with due respect, but more so because there is less room for error or inaccuracy and fewer escape options.

Single-engine flight at night can be quite safe. Some pilots tell tales of engine noises, fluctuating oil pressure, and rough running at night or over the sea, but the engine does not know that it is night, or that it is over mountains or water. So why does it seem to make strange noises? I don't know—perhaps we hear what isn't there because of heightened sensitivity. If you know the engine's maintenance history and have personally checked the fuel and oil, the engine should be very reliable. However, realize that a forced landing may not be an option in some areas. Choose your route with this in mind. A track with rivers, beaches, lakes, or straight, lit highways gives some chance of survival. Your autopilot, attitude indicator, and turn coordinator become as important as the engine. A powerful and reliable engine is useless if you have no attitude reference.

Night flight in a multi-engine airplane is potentially safer than in a single-engine one. However, engine failure and asymmetric control at night are demanding exercises in themselves, especially immediately after takeoff. Do not forget your emergency self-brief for these possibilities.

Equally important is the built-in redundancy in the lighting, electrical, and instrument systems. Unless you are current, confident, and competent at partial panel instrument flight, choose an airplane with a standby attitude indicator, if available.

Night "Visual" Flight

Night flight *is not* visual flight despite being called night VFR and the weather conditions being called night VMC. The official definition of night flight relates to weather conditions or to regulations and rules that apply, but not to the techniques of controlling the airplane.

This book highlights the *hows* and the *how nots* for safe night flight. Use the autopilot—it can be a good friend, but unlike your best friend, do not trust it absolutely. Keep a weather eye. The same advice applies to the GPS.

If you fly smoothly, confidently, and regularly, you will enjoy night flying.

Part 1

Refresher

Chapter 1

Instruments and Systems

The definitions and regulations regarding day visual meteorological conditions (VMC) and night VMC do not specify a clearly defined horizon. Night flight is instrument flight—make no mistake. If there is no visual horizon, you are flying on the clocks. During the day in reduced visibility and over level terrain, you may get away with a vertical reference below the airplane as a guide to airplane attitude and flight path. At night, it is too risky. Uneven distribution of lights and stars gives subtle but misleading cues as to which way is up, which way is down, and whether or not the airplane is level. You must fly attitude on instruments and be able to do so competently when talking on the radio, reading charts, writing down instructions, and looking for ground features and other traffic.

Flight instruments fall functionally into three categories: *pressure instruments, gyroscopic instruments*, and *compass instruments*. Pressure instruments include the airspeed indicator (ASI), the altimeter, and the vertical speed indicator (VSI). Gyroscopic instruments include the attitude indicator (AI), the heading indicator (HI), and the turn indicator or turn coordinator. Compass instruments use a magnetic reference. In support of the flight instruments are the pitot-static system, the vacuum system, and the electrical system. All of these are brought together by the greatest aid to the pilot—the autopilot.

Pressure Instruments

Airspeed Indicator

The *airspeed indicator* displays *indicated airspeed* (IAS). Indicated airspeed is a measure of dynamic pressure, which is the difference between the total pressure of the pitot head and the ambient static pressure. The airspeed indicator will have the following specific speeds marked on it:

- V_{S0}—stall speed at maximum weight, landing gear down, flaps down, power off;
- V_{S1}—stall speed at maximum weight, landing gear up, flaps up, power off;
- V_{FE}—maximum speed, flaps extended;
- V_{NO}—maximum structural cruise speed (for normal operations); and
- V_{NE}—never-exceed speed (maximum speed, all operations).

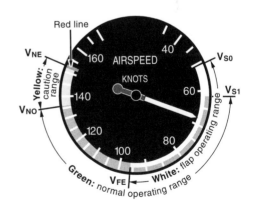

Figure 1-1 ASI.

In addition to showing indicated airspeed, some airspeed indicators are able to show *true airspeed* (TAS). These ASIs have a manually rotatable scale to set *outside air temperature* (OAT) against altitude, allowing the pilot to read TAS as well as IAS.

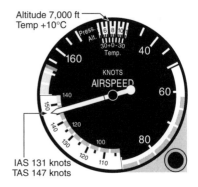

Altitude 7,000 ft
Temp +10°C

IAS 131 knots
TAS 147 knots

Figure 1-2 IAS/TAS indicator.

Airspeed Indicator Errors

Density Error

Density error occurs any time an airplane is flying in conditions that are other than *standard atmospheric conditions* (ISA) at sea level. This is why the airspeed indicator does not indicate TAS.

Compressibility Error

Compressibility error increases with airspeed but is only relevant above 200 knots.

Position Error

Position error occurs because of pitot-static system errors. Errors vary with speed and attitude and include maneuver-induced errors. *Pressure error correction* (PEC) is shown in the pilot's operating handbook. Indicated airspeed corrected for pressure and instrument error is called *calibrated airspeed* (CAS).

Instrument Error

Instrument error is caused by small manufacturing imperfections and the large mechanical amplification necessary for small, sensed movements. Instrument error is insignificant in general aviation (GA) airplanes.

Altimeter

The altimeter converts static pressure at the level of the airplane to register vertical distance from a *datum* (the reference from which a measurement is made). At lower altitudes, a one inch decrease in pressure indicates approximately 1,000 feet gain in altitude. For all operations in the U.S. below 18,000 feet, the local altimeter setting is used. Since the height of terrain and obstacles shown on a chart is above *mean sea level* (MSL), this becomes your altitude reference. At or above 18,000 feet MSL, standard pressure (29.92 in. Hg) is set and flight levels are reported to the nearest 100 feet (e.g. 11,500 feet is FL115), although cruising levels are usually whole thousands of feet (e.g. FL120). For all operations below 18,000 feet (the *transition altitude*), pilots are required to use the current local altimeter setting and then set 29.92 in. Hg when climbing through 18,000 feet. The setting is changed from standard pressure to the local altimeter setting when descending through FL180 (the *transition level*).

At or above 18,000 feet MSL, set 29.92 in. Hg in the pressure window. Below 18,000 feet MSL, set the local altimeter setting in the pressure window.

Altimeter Errors

Barometric Error

Barometric error is induced in an altimeter when atmospheric pressure at sea level differs from standard atmospheric conditions. The correct setting of the barometric subscale removes the error.

Figure 1-3 Altimeter.

Temperature Error

Temperature error is induced when the temperature (density) differs from standard atmospheric conditions. Note that there is no adjustment.

Position Error

Position error occurs because of static system errors and is minor. Errors vary with speed and attitude and include maneuver-induced errors.

Instrument Error

Instrument error is caused by small manufacturing imperfections and is insignificant.

Lag

Lag occurs when the response of the capsule and linkage is not instantaneous. The altimeter reading lags slightly when altitude is increased or decreased rapidly.

Altimeter Check

Whenever an accurate local altimeter setting is available and the airplane is at an airfield with a known elevation, pilots must conduct an accuracy check of the altimeter before takeoff. The altimeter is checked by comparing its indicated altitude to a known elevation using an accurate local altimeter setting. The altimeter should indicate site elevation within 75 feet; if it doesn't, have a mechanic inspect the altimeter prior to takeoff.

When operating out of a tower-controlled airport, you will have access to an accurate local altimeter setting; however, you may need to make an allowance for the difference between the airfield reference point and the position of your airplane at the time. Basically, a local altimeter setting that is provided by a tower, ATIS or remote-reporting airfield sensor can be considered accurate.

Vertical Speed Indicator

The *vertical speed indicator* (VSI) indicates the rate of change of altitude. The VSI is more sensitive to static pressure changes than the altimeter, and so it responds more quickly to an altitude change. However, there will always be some lag. Its principle of operation depends on lag. Generally, the trend is obvious almost immediately, but the precise rate will take a few seconds to be indicated. With large and sudden attitude changes, the VSI may briefly show a reversed reading before a steady rate of climb or descent is indicated because of disturbed airflow near the static vent. This is also likely in rough air. The lag can last as long as several seconds before the rate can be read—therefore fly attitude; be careful not to chase the VSI needle.

Figure 1-4 Vertical speed indicator (VSI).

Gyroscopic Instruments

Attitude Indicator

The *attitude indicator* (AI) is the only instrument that gives a direct and immediate picture of the pitch and bank of the airplane. You should become familiar with the specific attitudes you need to select and maintain for your airplane.

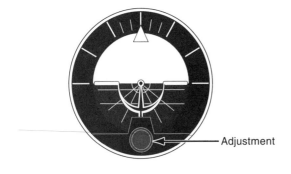

Figure 1-5 Pitch attitude.

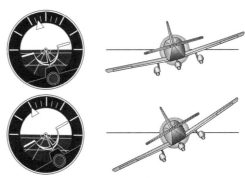

Fifteen and thirty degrees left

Figure 1-6 Bank attitude.

Attitude Indicator Errors

The attitude indicator is a reliable and accurate instrument. However, it may be subject to failures of the gyroscope drive system and precession errors.

If the AI suffers a failure of its rotor drive, it will become unstable. An electrically driven AI will usually have a warning flag to alert you of a power failure. If a power failure occurs, the AI will be unreliable and provide false attitude information. A failure in a vacuum-driven AI will produce the same result. To guard against this, you must monitor the suction gauge at regular intervals to ensure that an adequate vacuum pressure of between 3 and 5 inches of Hg is being provided.

The AI suffers from errors during sustained accelerations and turns because the erection switch senses a false vertical. A linear acceleration will exert g-forces that affect the self-erecting mechanism of the AI. During a rapid acceleration, as can occur at takeoff, the gravity sensors on the bottom of the gyroscope tend to get left behind and cause the gyroscope to precess forward at the top, moving the horizon bar down slightly producing a false indication of a climb. It responds just like its pilot's inner ear, and acceleration is sensed as a tilt (*somatogravic illusion*). These can cause false indications of pitch attitude and bank angle. The errors are usually small and are easily identified and corrected. Be careful immediately after a night takeoff to maintain a positive rate of climb.

Turn and Coordination Instruments

Coordination Ball/Inclinometer

If an airplane is not in coordinated flight, it will be either slipping or skidding. A curved glass tube filled with damping oil and containing a ball is provided to indicate slip or skid. It acts like a pendulum. The position of the ball is determined by the resultant of centrifugal reaction and gravity. The ball is not connected to the turn gyro.

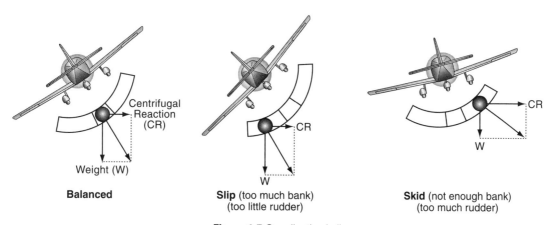

Figure 1-7 Coordination ball.

Turn Indicator/Turn Coordinator

On a turn indicator, the pointer is calibrated to show standard-rate—or rate-one—turns, left or right. A standard-rate turn causes the heading to change at 3° per second, hence a complete turn of 360° will take 2 minutes. Note that the wings are pivoted in the center and do not move up or down to indicate changes in pitch attitude. To avoid confusion with the attitude indicator, many turn coordinators are labeled with the warning, *no pitch information* (figure 1-9).

Figure 1-8 Turn indicator.

Figure 1-9 Turn coordinator.

Heading Indicator

The heading indicator (HI), sometimes referred to as the *directional gyro* (DG), is a directional instrument, but it has no inherent magnetic alignment. It contains a gyroscope powered by either a vacuum system or the electrical system. It relies on the pilot to manually align it with the magnetic compass after start and regularly in flight.

Heading Indicator Errors

The gyroscope in the HI does drift and needs to be realigned periodically (every 15 minutes). In flight, the airplane must be straight and level and stabilized whenever the HI is being aligned.

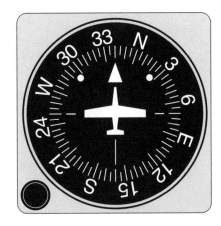

Figure 1-10 Heading indicator.

Compass Instruments

Magnetic Compass

The *magnetic compass*, or *direct indicating compass*, is the fundamental heading reference. In steady flight, magnetic heading appears under the *lubber line*, which indicates the nose of the airplane. Small errors in the reading will occur because of the influence of additional magnetic fields generated by the airplane and its components. A cockpit placard, known as the *deviation card* or *compass correction card* (figure 1-12), enables the pilot to allow for these errors. The deviation is very small. In straight-and-level, unaccelerated flight, the compass is accurate.

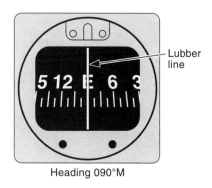

Figure 1-11
Magnetic compass.

DEVIATION CARD					
FOR					
N	30	60	E	120	150
STEER					
001	031	060	089	118	149
FOR					
S	210	240	W	300	330
STEER					
181	213	242	271	301	330
ON ☒ RADIOS ☐ OFF					

Figure 1-12
Deviation card (compass correction card).

The indications of the direct indicating compass are subject to significant errors when the airplane is turning (especially through north or south), and when accelerating (especially on east and west). These errors arise because of the adverse effect of *magnetic dip*, which is caused by the vertical component of the earth's magnetic field. The indications can also be misread as the direction to turn appears in reverse.

Remote Indicating Compass

A *remote indicating compass* combines the functions of the magnetic compass and the heading indicator. It employs a magnetic sensor, called a *flux valve* or a *magnetic flux detector*, that is positioned well away from other magnetic influences in the airframe, usually in a wing tip.

The sensor detects the earth's magnetic field and sends electrical signals to the gyro to automatically align it and therefore show the correct magnetic heading of the airplane. This process is known as *slaving*. It eliminates the need to manually realign the HI.

There is usually a small slaving knob on the instrument to allow the pilot to manually align the compass card quickly if the indicated heading is grossly in error. A small slaving annunciator is usually provided to assist manual alignment and allow the pilot to check that normal automatic slaving is occurring. This is indicated by small, regular oscillations of the slaving needle. Alignment is also cross-checked with the magnetic compass.

The gyro-stabilized magnetic compass is also used to drive the compass card in the *radio magnetic indicator* (RMI). Navigation information is superimposed on the heading indication (figure 1-13).

The more modern *horizontal situation indicator* (HSI) also presents a gyro-stabilized magnetic heading on a rotating card (figure 1-14). This may be presented with other useful guidance information on a mechanical instrument or an electronic display as part of an *electronic flight instrumentation system* (EFIS).

Figure 1-13
Radio magnetic indicator with heading
"bug" at the top and two ADF needles.

Figure 1-14
Horizontal situation indicator.

Other Instruments

Clock
One of the most important instruments for night operations is the clock, which is often placed on the control column. Make sure you are familiar with the functions of the clock, whether digital or analog, before going night flying. As pilot in command, you should get into the habit of always wearing a suitable watch which indicates hours, minutes, and seconds. There should also be a stopwatch (elapsed time) function.

Timer
A very useful pilot aid which is standard in IFR aircraft, and which I think should be fitted to all aircraft, is a combined digital clock/timer. It is used for absolute and elapsed time and is very useful for both visual and instrument approaches and measuring progress along track.

Preflight Checks of the Flight Instruments

During the preflight inspection, check that the pitot cover is removed and that the pitot tube and the static vents are not obstructed in any way. To check the pitot heating system, switch on the master switch and pitot heat. Carefully feel the pitot tube with your fingers within 30 seconds of turning on the pitot heat. Check pitot heating with caution; the pitot heater is capable of burning your hand. Do not forget to switch the pitot heat off after testing. The pitot heat should not be left on for long periods on the ground.

When in the cockpit, check that all the glass coverings of the instruments are intact, the tube of the coordination ball contains fluid and the ball is at the lowest point, the magnetic compass contains fluid that is free of bubbles and not discolored, and the deviation card is in place.

After starting the engine and switching on the alternator, listen for any unusual mechanical noises as the gyros spin up. The airspeed indicator should indicate zero, the VSI should indicate zero, and the altimeter should indicate the airfield elevation to within 75 feet with the local altimeter setting used. Check that the clock is wound (if applicable), the correct time is set, and the stopwatch is functioning. When the gyros have erected, set the AI's miniature airplane against the horizon line and align the HI with the magnetic compass.

Check the vacuum gauge. There should be no red warning flags on the electrical gyroscopic instruments, and there should be sufficient suction (3 to 5 inches of Hg) for the suction-driven instruments—a suitable check would be: "*AI and HI erect and aligned, no flags, suction checked.*"

When taxiing, check the HI, turn coordinator, and the coordination ball during gentle turns:
- turning left, heading decreasing, skidding right, wings level, ADF needle tracking; and
- turning right, heading increasing, skidding left, wings level, ADF tracking.

If desired, the AI can be checked by gently applying the brakes until the nose drops slightly. At the holding point and when stationary, the HI can be realigned with the magnetic compass. On the runway, check that the heading and the runway direction are within 5°.

Pitot-Static System

You will recall that three flight instruments are connected to the pitot-static system:
- the airspeed indicator (static pressure and total pressure);
- the altimeter (static pressure only); and
- the vertical speed indicator (static pressure only).

Problems in the static system will affect all three pressure instruments. Problems in the pitot system will affect the airspeed indicator only.

The pitot tube measures total pressure, also known as *pitot pressure* or *ram air pressure*. The static vent, or static port, measures only static pressure. The difference is *dynamic pressure*.

Many airplanes have two static vents, one on each side of the fuselage, and this is known as a *balanced* static system. This reduces the errors caused by sideslip. Some airplanes have a combined pitot-static tube. An alternate static source may also be available in the event of a static system blockage, usually the static pressure within the cockpit. This static pressure is usually less than the external static pressure and will cause significant position error to the altimeter and ASI. There is normally a correction table in the flight manual if the alternate static source is used.

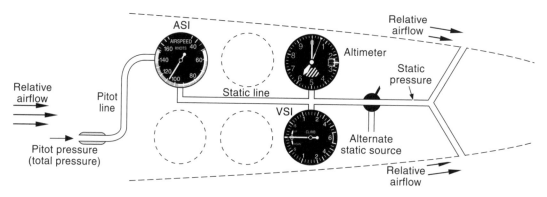

Figure 1-15 Pitot-static system.

Blockage of a Static Vent

In a climb with a blocked static vent, the altimeter will indicate a constant altitude, the VSI will indicate zero, and the ASI will underread because of the trapped static pressure being greater than the ambient static pressure. In a descent with a blocked static vent, the altimeter reading will not change, the VSI will indicate zero, and the ASI will overread. This can be dangerous, as a descent into high terrain could occur without the descent being indicated by the altimeter and VSI. The pilot could also react to the over-reading ASI by reducing speed and inadvertently stalling the airplane. This reinforces the value of knowing the power/attitude combinations for your airplane.

Blockage of the Pitot Tube

If the pitot tube is blocked, only the ASI is affected. The pitot tube is particularly vulnerable to icing because of its position in the airflow, hence airplanes have a pitot heater to prevent ice formation. The pitot heater should be on whenever the airplane is operating in visible moisture (e.g. cloud, mist, rain) with an OAT at or below +10°C, and at all times when the OAT is less than 0°C.

If the pitot tube becomes blocked, the total pressure in the tube will remain constant at that value. Therefore, as the static pressure reduces in a climb, the airspeed indicator will overread. Conversely, the airspeed indicator will underread in a descent. For example, if the pitot heat is left off and ice forms during the climb, the airspeed reading will increase progressively, and the pilot will be tempted to raise the nose to reduce speed, thereby risking a stall.

Remember to always set attitude and power. Whenever the airplane is to be parked for an extended period, a pitot cover should be used. Do not forget that wasps and other insects can block a pitot tube.

Vacuum System

Gyroscopes that are vacuum powered have the instrument casing partially evacuated by an engine-driven pump. Air is drawn into the instrument case and directed at high speed to the gyro rotor. A common arrangement has the attitude indicator and the HI driven by suction and the turn indicator or turn coordinator driven electrically. Alternatively, an electrically driven standby attitude indicator is installed—a much safer option.

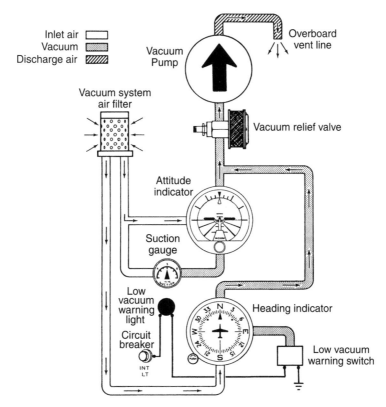

Figure 1-16 Typical vacuum system.

With a loss of electrical power, the turn coordinator could be lost, but the attitude indicator would still be available. With a loss of suction, the attitude indicator could gradually become erratic and then fail completely, but the turn coordinator would remain serviceable.

However, it is possible for an individual instrument to fail because of an internal fault rather than a power supply problem. The suction gauge should be checked periodically. Power failure to an electrically driven gyroscope is usually indicated by a red warning flag on the affected instrument(s).

Electrical System

The electrical system powers the lights, radios, NAVAIDs, and engine starter, but not the engine ignition (spark plugs). The electrical power is either 14 or 28 volts DC and is connected directly to a *bus bar*. The bus bar distributes all the electrical power. The current then flows through a return wire attached to the airplane's metal structure to complete the circuit. Composite structures have a separate earth return wire.

Alternator

As well as providing the power for lights, radios, and other services, a very important function of the alternator is to recharge the battery. Some airplanes have a warning light that illuminates when the engine rpm is insufficient for the alternator to charge. When taxiing with lights and NAVAIDs on, you may need to set 1,200 rpm or so (more than idle rpm).

Battery

Although the engine ignition is independent of the electrical system, other services—such as lights, radios, and perhaps flaps—are not. The battery is the electrical life belt. *Do not fly at night with a less than fully charged battery.*

Autopilot

The autopilot is a vital element of night VFR. It is another tool available to the competent pilot, and it is designed to relieve pilot workload so that the pilot can concentrate on situational awareness and flight management.

Roles of the Autopilot

A very simple autopilot may only provide limited hands-free operation in the form of the following:
- *flight stabilization* in one or more axes;
- *maneuver control* through holding a heading, altitude, or attitude setting; and
- *system coupling* in following a NAVAID or course command.

The autopilot provides these services by taking information from attitude, performance, and navigation sensors, assembling the data, and responding in accordance with the pilot's settings. The autopilot has the additional means of physically moving the control surfaces to achieve the desired flight path. The first autopilots, nicknamed *George*, were attached to the control column and physically actuated the controls as if the pilot were flying. Now with electrically signaled, electromechanical or hydraulically operated controls, the autopilot has become simple, small, and reliable, and autopilot modes have become the primary means of piloting the airplane.

Sensors

Attitude Sensing

An autopilot system senses and maintains attitude with reference to a gyroscopic horizon. It literally flies on instruments, just as a pilot would in cloud or at night.

There are two types of gyros that are relevant:
- a rate gyro, which senses angular movement or deviations, roll or yaw; and
- an attitude gyro, which provides pitch and roll attitude.

Roll and Yaw Rate

The turn coordinator is used in basic autopilots to provide the roll and yaw rate signals and therefore functions as the sensor for the basic, *wings-leveler* autopilot, i.e. it quickly senses any deviation.

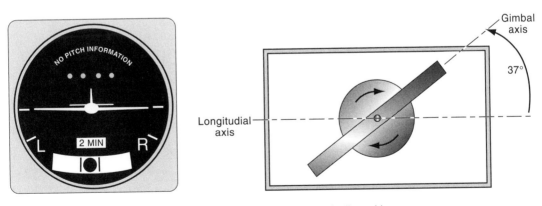

Figure 1-17 Turn coordinator—yaw and roll sensitive.

Attitude

The attitude indicator uses a vertical gyroscope, the rotor of which is kept vertical, or erect, by gravity-sensing devices on the bottom of the unit. By fitting electronic pick-ups to this vertical gyro, an electrical signal representing both pitch and roll attitude can be provided to the autopilot.

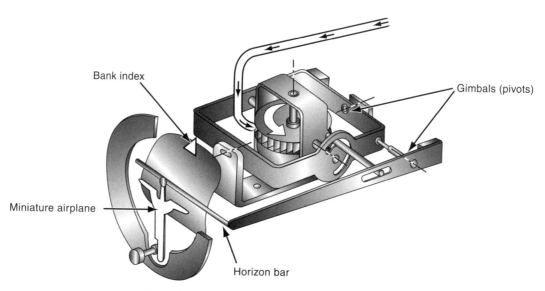

Figure 1-18 Attitude indicator—pitch and roll sensitive.

Stabilization (Inner Loop)

With the autopilot engaged, any deviation in roll (or pitch) causes an error signal to be generated, and the appropriate response must occur. The computer amplifies the signal and sends it to the *servo*. This servo is the power (muscle) that will cause aileron displacement. The airplane responds, and when the wings are level, the error signal is cancelled.

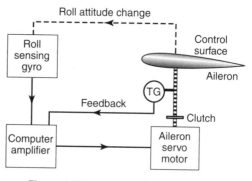

Figure 1-19 Inner loop of a single channel.

Control

The autopilot provides the airplane with an automatic flight stabilization and error correction system. Should the airplane be displaced from its gyroscopic reference, it will be returned to that reference. For control, the stabilization is temporarily overridden to allow appropriate control surface movements to induce the required maneuvers. It is the same as the *control* system having to overcome the *stability* of the airplane.

The pilot now commands the autopilot to turn left. This can be done with *control-wheel steering* (CWS) or a rotary roll (bank) control switch, or by setting a desired heading. The autopilot then produces a false error signal, which is the equivalent of the airplane banking to the right, to the inner loop.

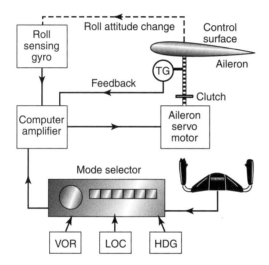

Figure 1-20
Inner and outer loop of a
single channel.

System Coupling

Some very useful autopilot modes are made available by maneuver control and system coupling. After the autopilot is engaged, push buttons allow the pilot to select various modes. The selected mode is indicated on the annunciator. Autopilot modes depend on the complexity of the system, e.g. airspeed hold, altitude hold, localizer track, or ILS glide slope. Some also have auto-throttles.

Additional Autopilot Features

Rotary Roll Switch

The *rotary roll switch* overrides the wings leveler and allows the pilot to turn the airplane to a desired heading or perhaps to make an orbit (a complete 360° turn). When the knob is centered, the airplane will be returned to wings-level. An arrow on the RMI or HSI shows the selected heading. The knob has a central, spring-loaded detent.

Electric Trim

While not a subsystem of the autopilot, electric trim is often installed. It simply provides a means of electrically driving the trim tab to relieve control pressures. A spring-loaded, self-centring switch, which moves fore and aft in the same sense as the control column, activates an electric motor that drives the manual trim system. Some airplanes have very powerful electric trims, and if they malfunction, they can require considerable force to control them.

Note. Electric trim, like an autopilot, is usually reliable, but it can malfunction. Although you can physically overpower the autopilot, it is essential to know the location of the autopilot disconnect switch and electric trim circuit breaker so that either system can be switched off should they not behave as designed.

Limitations of the Autopilot

There are specific limitations on all autopilots in light airplanes; the flight manual autopilot supplement is the best reference. Typically:

- during climb or descent, it is not permitted to operate the autopilot below 200 feet AGL; and
- in the cruise, it is not permitted to operate the autopilot below 1,000 feet AGL.

All modern autopilots have a built-in, self-test function. The autopilot must not be engaged in flight unless it has been tested before flight on that day.

Chapter 2

Meteorology

Generally, at night it is difficult to see clouds, and there are restrictions to visibility, particularly on dark nights or in overcast conditions. The VFR pilot must exercise caution to avoid flying into clouds or a layer of fog. Usually, the first indication of flying into restricted visibility conditions is the gradual disappearance of lights on the ground. If the lights begin to take on an appearance of being surrounded by a halo or glow, use caution in attempting further flight in that same direction. Such a halo or glow around lights on the ground is indicative of ground fog. If a descent must be made through fog, smoke, or haze in order to land, the horizontal visibility is considerably less when looking through the restriction than it is when looking straight down through it from above. Under no circumstances should a VFR night flight be made during poor or marginal weather conditions unless both the pilot and aircraft are certificated and equipped for flight under instrument flight rules (IFR). It is especially important to fly with current weather information at night; update your forecasts and weather reports frequently while en route.

Clouds

The type of precipitation depends on the type of cloud from which it falls. Rain, snow, or hail falling as showers comes from cumuliform clouds, with the heaviest rain showers falling from cumulonimbus. Non-showery precipitation, on the other hand, usually falls from stratiform cloud, mainly altostratus or nimbostratus. It is therefore possible to use precipitation as a means of identifying cloud type.

Figure 2-1 Non-showery (i.e. steady) precipitation from stratiform clouds.

Non-showery precipitation, such as steady rain, light snow, or drizzle, fall from stratiform clouds, mainly altostratus and nimbostratus (figure 2-1). Rain or snow showers generally fall from cumuliform clouds (figure 2-2). Since you won't be able to see the clouds during night flight, you will need to rely on other factors to determine the conditions you are flying in.

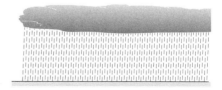

Figure 2-2
Showers fall from cumuliform clouds.

Grouping of Clouds

Clouds are described according to a system of classification derived from four main forms which indicate cloud appearance:

- *cumulus* (or cumulo-) are heaped-type clouds;
- *stratus* (or strato-) are layer-type clouds;
- *nimbus* (or nimbo-) has a dark, dense appearance (suggesting heavy moisture) and are rain-producing clouds; and
- *cirrus* (or cirro-) has a hair-like or fibrous appearance.

Clouds are further classified by the height of the base of a cloud *above ground level* (AGL). The height of an individual cloud base falls into one of three groups (note that these height ranges can vary with latitude):

- low, which is less than 6,500 feet AGL;
- middle, which is 6,500 to 20,000 feet AGL; and
- high, which is above 20,000 feet AGL.

Clouds with vertical development, known as *convective clouds*, are also described. There are ten main cloud groups, and their abbreviations and height groupings are given in table 2-1.

Cloud Group	Abbreviation	Cloud Height
stratus	St	Low-level cloud
stratocumulus	Sc	Low-level cloud
nimbostratus	Ns	Low-level cloud
cumulus	Cu	Low-level cloud with vertical development
cumulonimbus	Cb	Low-level cloud with vertical development
altostratus	As	Middle-level cloud
altocumulus	Ac	Middle-level cloud
cirrus	Ci	High-level cloud
cirrostratus	Cs	High-level cloud
cirrocumulus	Cc	High-level cloud

Table 2-1 The ten main groups of clouds.

Note. Other Latin terms, such as *fractus* (broken), *lenticularis* (lens shaped), *mammatus* (bulbous), and *castellanus* (towering) are used to describe sub-categories of these main cloud groups.

Cloud and Air Stability

The structure or type of cloud that forms depends mainly on the stability of the air. When unstable moist air is lifted by any means, it will continue rising, forming heaped-type (*cumuliform*) cloud with significant vertical development and turbulence. On the other hand, stable moist air has no tendency to continue rising and will form layer-type (*stratiform*) cloud with little or no turbulence. Some layer-type cloud, such as nimbostratus, can form in a very deep layer (10,000 feet or more). Air that is forced to rise (i.e. orographic) but which does not cool to its *dewpoint* (i.e. the temperature at which water vapor condenses) will not condense to form clouds.

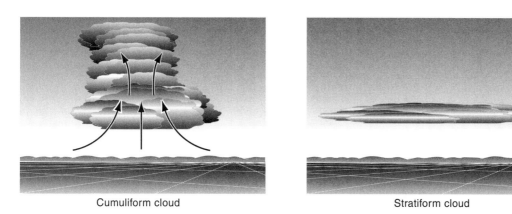

| Cumuliform cloud | Stratiform cloud |

Figure 2-3 Cumulus cloud forms in unstable conditions, and stratus cloud forms in stable conditions.

Unstable Air

So long as a vertically moving parcel of air remains warmer than its surroundings, it will continue to rise. This is known as an *unstable parcel of air*. This can give rise to a current of rising air called a *thermal*.

Characteristics of unstable air include:
- turbulence in the rising air, especially in thermals;
- the formation of cumuliform clouds (i.e. heaped clouds);
- showery rain (precipitation); and
- good visibility between the showers (the rising air carries pollutants away in it).

Stable Air

When a rising parcel of air achieves the same temperature as that of the ambient air, it will stop rising, because its density will be the same as that of the surroundings. An atmosphere in which air tends to remain at the one level is called a *stable atmosphere*.

Characteristics of stable air include:

- the formation of stratiform clouds (i.e. layer-type cloud);
- steady precipitation, if any;
- poor visibility if there are any obscuring particles; and
- the likelihood of smooth flying conditions with little or no turbulence.

There could be an inversion, which traps pollution and reduces visibility. Fog may also result.

Formation of Clouds

Clouds are formed when moist air is forced to rise, and then it condenses. The various means (called triggers or *stimuli*) of causing the vertical motion of a parcel of air include:

- convection (or thermal turbulence);
- orographic lift (i.e. the forced uplift of air over high ground);
- turbulence and mixing; and
- slow, widespread ascent of an air mass (e.g. a cold front).

Precipitation

Types of Precipitation

Precipitation refers to falling water that finally reaches the ground. It includes:

- rain, which consists of liquid water drops;
- drizzle, which consists of fine water droplets significantly smaller in size than raindrops and falls from a continuous and dense layer of low stratus cloud;
- snow, which falls as branched and star-shaped ice crystals;
- hail, which falls as balls of ice; and
- freezing rain or freezing drizzle, which consists of water drops or droplets that freeze on contact with a cold surface, such as the ground or an airplane in flight.

Note. Rain that does not reach the ground is called *virga*.

Intensity of Precipitation

The intensity of precipitation, regardless of its type, can be described as light, moderate, or heavy. These three terms have different codes and abbreviations in weather forecasts. Precipitation can fall either as showers, or as intermittent or continuous rain, snow, or drizzle.

Showers are characterized by sudden stopping and starting, and they are subject to rapid and sometimes violent changes in intensity. The cloud is quite likely to break up, or even clear, between the showers.

Intermittent precipitation in the form of rain, snow, or drizzle is not continual at the surface of the earth, even though there is no break in the associated cloud. Intermittent precipitation differs from showers in that it does not start or stop suddenly, and there is no clearing of the cloud between the periods of precipitation.

Thunderstorms

Characteristics of Thunderstorms

A thunderstorm is storm cloud with one or more sudden electrical discharges, evidenced by a flash of light (lightning) and a sharp rumbling sound (thunder). The noise known as thunder is the sound of the lightning discharge. As the speed of light is much faster than the speed of sound, lightning is seen some time before thunder is heard. When these two phenomena appear to be simultaneous, the close proximity of a thunderstorm is indicated. Thunderstorms are associated with cumulonimbus clouds only and generate spectacular and dangerous weather, often accompanied by heavy rain, hail, squalls, microbursts, and windshear.

In its mature stage, the top of a storm cloud can reach up as far as the tropopause, which is around 36,000 feet above the earth's surface in temperate latitudes, and 55,000 feet in the tropics. The mature storm cloud may have the typical shape of a cumulonimbus, with the top spreading out in an *anvil* shape in the direction of the upper winds.

The mature stage of a thunderstorm typically lasts between 20 and 40 minutes and is characterized by updrafts, downdrafts, and precipitation. There is so much water falling through the cloud toward the end of the mature stage that it starts to wash out the updrafts. The forces are greatest just before the storm breaks (i.e. just before heavy rain starts to fall).

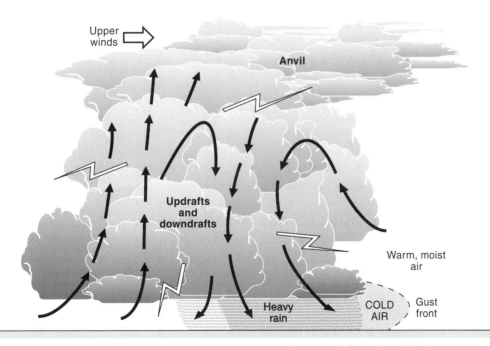

Figure 2-4 The mature stage is characterized by updrafts, downdrafts, and precipitation.

It is possible for an updraft of, say, 4,000 fpm to be adjacent to a downdraft also of 4,000 fpm, resulting in a shear of 8,000 fpm. As the cold downdrafts flow out of the base of the cloud at a great rate, they change direction and begin to flow horizontally. On approaching the ground, the strong downdrafts tend to spread out in all directions, with the forward edge in front of the cloud forming a *gust front*. Strong windshear will occur, and this has caused the demise of many airplanes, large and small.

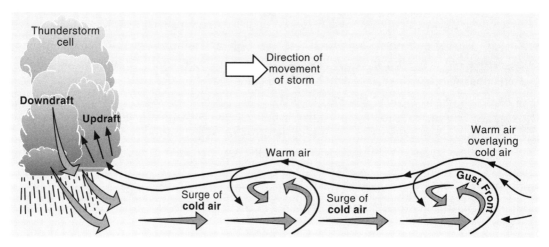

Figure 2-5 Cross section of a typical gust front.

The outflowing cold air will undercut the inflowing warmer air, and new storm cells can form. A gusty wind and a sudden drop in temperature may precede a storm. A roll cloud may also develop at the base of the main cloud where the cold downdrafts and warm updrafts pass, indicating possible extreme turbulence.

Hailstones

Large hailstones often form inside cumulonimbus clouds as water adheres to already formed hailstones and then freezes, leading to even larger hailstones. In certain conditions, hailstones can grow to the size of oranges. Almost all cumulonimbus clouds contain hail, most of which melts before reaching the ground, where it falls as rain.

Downbursts and Microbursts

Strong downdrafts that spread out near the ground are known as *downbursts*. A very strong downburst not exceeding 2½ miles in diameter is called a *microburst*.

A typical microburst has the following dimensions:
• horizontal distance of 2½ miles;
• lifetime of 10 minutes;
• horizontal windshear of 50 knots; and
• vertical depth of cold air outflow of 1,000–4,000 feet.

Airplanes may not have the performance capability or the structural strength to combat the extremely strong downdrafts, turbulence, and windshear in downbursts and microbursts. Many airplanes have crashed as a result.

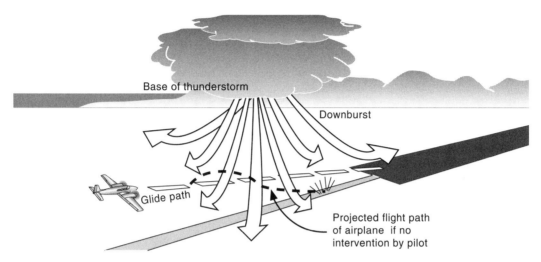

Figure 2-6 Landing through a downburst results in a change of flight path.

Downbursts and microbursts are often associated with cumulonimbus clouds, but they may also occur with any heat cloud, such as cumulus cloud, or with clouds from which virga is falling. As rain falls from high cloud and evaporates (i.e. virga), it absorbs latent heat and creates a very cold parcel of air that may plummet toward the ground as a downburst or a microburst. In extreme cases, microbursts have been known to blow hundreds of trees down in a radial pattern and to blow trains off rails.

Microbursts and downbursts may appear very suddenly and may or may not last very long. Even though one airplane might make a satisfactory approach underneath a large cloud, a following airplane may not.

Despite the general lack of illumination at night, it is often possible to detect the shape and structure of cloud formations by the stars and lights that are obscured. Be particularly wary of cloud formations that have vertical development. Try to track directly towards clearly defined lights. Any electrical activity is very visible at night. Stay clear.

The density of the cloud is also noticeable from the reflections of your own navigation lights and strobes. The more solid the cloud, the more solid the turbulence and precipitation.

You may also notice an unusual phenomenon called St. Elmo's fire. In very dry air near thunderstorms, the static electricity within the aircraft structure builds and may discharge as dancing lights on the windscreen or canopy frame. It is not hazardous but can be distracting.

Windshear

Windshear is defined as a change in wind direction and/or wind speed over a limited horizontal and/or vertical distance. Any changes in wind velocity or direction as you move from one point to another is a windshear. The stronger the changes and the shorter the distance within which they occur, the stronger the windshear.

There are many causes of windshear. They include:

- obstructions and terrain features that disrupt the normal smooth wind flow close to the ground; and
- localized vertical air movements associated with thunderstorms, cumulonimbus, and other large cumuliform clouds, such as gust fronts, downbursts, and microbursts, with the windshear formed from updrafts and downdrafts regarded as the most hazardous.

The term *low-level windshear* is used to specify any windshear occurring near the ground in the vicinity of the final approach path, runway, or takeoff/initial climb areas. Windshear near the ground (i.e. below about 3,000 feet) can be hazardous.

Storm Hazards to Aviation

Thunderstorms present a severe and potentially lethal hazard to aviation, and they must be treated with the utmost respect. Moreover, the dangers to aviation from a thunderstorm do not exist only inside and under the storm cloud, but also for quite some distance around it. Strong wind currents associated with thunderstorms may throw hailstones well out from the core of the storm, possibly several miles, where they may fall in clear air.

Thunderstorms are best avoided by at least 10 NM and, in severe situations, by perhaps 20 NM or more. Diverting downwind of a storm should be avoided.

The violent updrafts and downdrafts (which are very close to each other in a mature thunderstorm) cause extremely strong vertical windshear and turbulence, which can cause structural failure of the airframe. The rapidly changing direction from which the airflow strikes the wings could also cause a stall. Flying into a mature cumulonimbus cloud is very risky. The greatest turbulence within the cloud is found in the lower to middle part of the storm around the freezing level.

Most advanced airplanes are equipped with weather radar and/or stormscopes which enable pilots to identify the position of storm cells. Without weather radar, a pilot is forced to use eyesight and common sense. However, it will be difficult to see a storm if it is embedded and rising out of a general cloud base or out of layers of cloud that obscure storm clouds. Frequent lightning from within a cumulonimbus cloud, the presence of rain cloud, and the presence of a roll cloud indicate a severe thunderstorm. SIGMETs are issued to warn pilots of active thunderstorm areas and other meteorological hazards.

Some obvious dangers to airplanes from thunderstorms include:
- severe windshear, which may cause large flight path deviations and handling problems, loss of airspeed, and possible structural damage;
- severe turbulence, which may cause a loss of control and possible structural damage;
- severe icing, possibly the very dangerous clear ice that forms from large, supercooled water drops striking a below-freezing surface;
- hail damage to the airframe and cockpit windows;
- reduced visibility;
- damage from lightning strikes, including electrical damage; and
- interference to communications and navigation instruments.

The most severe flying conditions, such as heavy hail and destructive winds, may be produced in a *line squall*, which is a non-frontal band of very active thunderstorms, possibly in a long line that requires a large detour to fly around. This line (or sometimes more than one line) of thunderstorms can form in the relatively warm air ahead of a cold front and can be quite fast moving. A line squall may contain a number of severe thunderstorms, destructive winds, heavy hail, and possible tornadoes and can present a most intense hazard to airplanes.

Avoiding Thunderstorms

Thunderstorm activity is often scattered, making it easier for a pilot to avoid individual cells. Sometimes there may be a line of thunderstorms associated with, for instance, a cold front. There may be large, isolated thunderstorms, or there may be a whole line of them. The Stormscope makes for a critical component to your night panel if you intend to fly during conditions conducive to storms.

When diverting to avoid a thunderstorm, it is generally better to track upwind of the storm by at least 10 NM, where there is less likelihood of severe turbulence and hail. If there is intense thunderstorm activity in your flight plan area, it may be advisable to postpone your flight until the thunderstorm activity has ceased. If in flight, divert to a nearby suitable airfield, land, and wait until the thunderstorm activity has passed or ceased.

Night flight is safest above all cloud where you can see the stars and therefore stay clear of build-ups. However, navigation relies on NAVAIDs, and you need to be sure that the destination weather allows a free descent. If you have to transit through or below clouds, there should be some indication of the potential hazards in terms of electrical activity, precipitation and turbulence. As soon as these symptoms appear, consider a deviation in track or change of altitude.

Do not fly under thunderstorms as you may encounter hazards such as severe turbulence, strong downdrafts, microbursts, heavy hail, or windshear. If there is a possibility of approaching the edge of a thunderstorm, the best course of action is to make a gentle 180° turn and head to the smoother air you left behind.

Turbulence Penetration Techniques

Sometimes turbulence cannot be avoided, and you need to fly the airplane in a manner that enables it to handle the turbulent conditions as well as possible. Slow down. Some airplanes have a turbulence penetration speed (V_B) specified in the pilot's operating handbook. You should reduce to below this speed, otherwise reduce to below the maneuvering speed (V_A). The turbulence penetration speed is an intermediate speed that will be fast enough to prevent a stall at the low end of the speed range but slow enough to avoid overstressing the airframe at the high end of the range. *Fly attitude.*

Maneuvering speed is higher when the airplane is heavy, so a well-laden airplane is more stable in turbulent air and less susceptible to overstressing because of gust loads. In turbulence, you should normally leave the landing gear in the retracted position and the flaps up, since the strength of the airframe is greater in this configuration.

If you cannot avoid flying through or near a thunderstorm, steer a heading that will take the least time, establish a power setting for turbulence penetration speed, turn on the pitot heaters and other anti-icing equipment, keep the wings level, and be prepared to allow the altitude to vary in updrafts and downdrafts. Avoid over controlling the elevators in turbulence as this may overstress the airframe structure. Hold the attitude rather than the altitude. If possible, avoid turns as they increase g-loading, and continue straight ahead. Allow the speed to fluctuate in turbulence, and avoid rapid power changes. Finally, report the presence, position, and extent of the thunderstorms, as well as severe turbulence and icing.

Air Masses and Fronts

Frontal Weather

Air Masses

An *air mass* is a large parcel of air with fairly consistent properties (such as temperature and moisture content) throughout. It is usual to classify air masses according to the following:
- origin;
- path over the earth's surface; and
- whether the air is diverging or converging.

Cold Front

A cold front occurs when a cooler air mass undercuts a mass of warm air and displaces it at the surface. On weather charts, the boundary between the two air masses at the surface is shown as a line with barbs pointing in the direction in which the *front* is travelling. The cold front moves quite rapidly, with the cooler frontal air at altitude lagging behind the air at the surface.

Air that is forced to rise with the passage of a cold front is unstable, and the changes in weather accompanying the passage of a cold front can be quite pronounced. Atmospheric pressure will fall as a cold front approaches, and when the front has passed, the pressure may rise rapidly. There may be cumulus cloud and possibly cumulonimbus cloud with heavy rain showers, thunderstorm activity, and squalls. A squall line may also form ahead of the front. There may be a sudden drop in temperature— the cooler air mass will contain less moisture than the warm air, and the dewpoint will be lower after the cold front has passed. There may

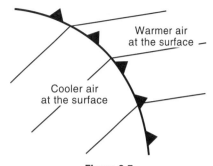

Figure 2-7
A cold front as depicted on a weather chart.

be low-level windshear as, or just after, the front approaches and a change in wind direction, with the direction shifting clockwise in the Northern Hemisphere (i.e. veering) and counterclockwise in the Southern Hemisphere (i.e. backing).

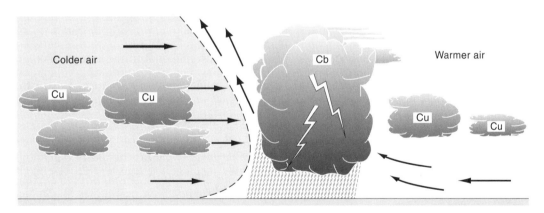

Figure 2-8 Cross section of a cold front.

Flying through a cold front may require diversions to avoid weather. There may be thunderstorm activity, violent winds (both horizontal and vertical) from cumulonimbus clouds, squall lines, windshear, heavy showers of rain or hail, or severe turbulence. Icing could also be a problem. Visibility away from showers and clouds may be quite good, but it is still a good idea to avoid the strong weather activity that can accompany cold fronts.

Icing

The Effects of Icing on Airplanes

Ice accretion on the airframe or within an engine induction system can have serious consequences for an airplane in flight. There can be adverse aerodynamic effects caused by ice building up on the airframe, resulting in a modification of the airflow pattern around airfoils (e.g. the wings or propeller blades). This can lead to a serious loss of lift and thrust and an increase in drag. If ice blocks the engine air intake in sub-zero temperatures or if carburetor ice forms in moist air up to +25°C, loss of engine power or even a complete engine failure can result. The airplane will increase in weight (ice is heavy), and there may be an unbalancing of control surfaces or of the propeller, perhaps causing severe vibration and control difficulties. Ice can block the pitot tube and/or static vent, producing errors in the pressure instruments. Radio communications and NAVAID performance can be affected if ice forms on the antennas, and the formation of ice on the windshield can reduce visibility.

Conditions Conducive to the Formation of Ice

For ice to form on the airframe, three general conditions need to exist:
- there must be visible moisture (cloud or rain);
- the outside air temperature must be at or below freezing (0°C); and
- the airframe temperature must be less than 0°C.

Note. At speeds above 300 KIAS, heating due to friction makes airframe icing unlikely.

Temperature decreases with increasing altitude (unless there is an inversion), often referred to as the *lapse rate*. The average lapse rate of temperature decrease is 2°C/1,000 feet. In standard conditions, you can apply the more accurate lapse rate of 3°C/1,000 feet for dry air, known as the *dry adiabatic lapse rate* (DALR), and 1.5°C/1,000 feet for clouds, known as the *saturated adiabatic lapse rate* (SALR). The *freezing level* is the altitude at which the ambient temperature is 0°C. For example, if the temperature is +8°C at 2,000 feet and the cloud base is at 4,000 feet, the freezing level would be just over 5,300 feet.

The worst icing conditions are usually found near the freezing level in heavy stratiform clouds or in rain. Icing is possible up to at least 8,000 feet but less common above this where droplets in clouds are already frozen. However, in cumuliform clouds with strong updrafts, large water droplets may be carried to higher altitudes, and this makes structural icing a possibility up to very high altitudes. Moreover, in cumuliform clouds, the freezing level is distorted upward in updrafts and downward in downdrafts, often by many thousands of feet. This leads to the potential for severe icing to occur at almost any level.

Airframe icing is most likely to accumulate rapidly in conditions of freezing rain (rain ice). This may occur at sub-zero temperatures underneath the face of a warm front with nimbostratus cloud from which rain is falling.

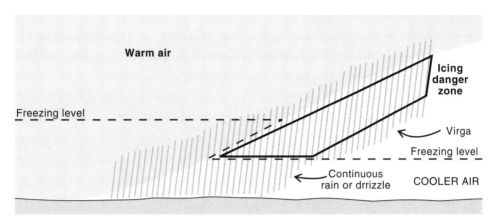

Figure 2-9 Danger area for icing beneath a warm front.

Types of Icing

Clear Ice

Clear ice is the most dangerous form of airframe icing. It is formed when a large water droplet has a temperature of just below 0°C. The droplet does not freeze all at once. Some of it freezes on impact, and the rest flows back over the airframe and freezes as it flows.

It is possible for liquid water drops to exist in the atmosphere at temperatures well below the normal freezing point of water (0°C), possibly at −15°C or even lower. This is referred to as *supercooled* water. One situation in which this can occur is when rain falls from air warmer than 0°C into a below-freezing layer of air beneath. Supercooled droplets are in an unstable state and will freeze on contact with a below-freezing surface, such as the skin of an airplane, the intakes, or the propeller blades (especially leading edges).

Figure 2-10 Clear ice is formed from large, supercooled water drops.

The freezing of each drop will be relatively gradual because of the latent heat released in the freezing process, which allows part of the water drop to spread rearward before it freezes. The slower the freezing process, the further the water drop will spread back before it freezes. This spreading back is greatest at temperatures just below 0°C. The result is a sheet of solid, clear, glazed ice with very little air enclosed. This makes clear ice difficult to remove.

The surface of clear ice is smooth, usually with undulations and lumps. Clear ice can alter the aerodynamic shape of airfoils quite dramatically and reduce or destroy airfoil effectiveness. Along with the increased weight, this creates a hazard to flight safety. Clear ice is very tenacious, and if it does break off, large chunks could damage the airframe.

A good indication that freezing rain may exist at higher altitudes is the presence of ice pellets. Ice pellets are formed by rain falling from warmer air and freezing on the way down through colder air, i.e. the presence of ice pellets usually indicates cold air that is below freezing (0°C) with a layer of warmer air above.

Wet snow is an indication of warmer air at your level and below-freezing temperatures at higher altitudes. The snow formed in the sub-zero temperatures of the air above melts to form wet snow as it passes through the warmer air near your level.

Be conscious of the possibility of ice whenever you are in moist air or cloud and close to freezing level. In a slower aircraft, the build-up can be quite quick (as there is no airframe heating due to speed), and the effect on performance may be significant. Ice adds considerable weight to the structure.

If the windows are foggy, the air is moist and the structure is cold. Therefore, there is also a risk of airframe icing. Always check for ice build up on your airframe by using your flashlight—but be careful to avoid its direct glare.

You may also note some increasing friction in the flight controls, if you are flying the airplane manually. If this happens, change direction clear of cloud or change altitude as soon as you safely can. Some airplanes have been lost due to frozen flight control surfaces and ice build up.

You may be able to climb above cloud to avoid icing, but be sure your airplane has the performance to transit through the icing levels during the climb. Mostly, you need to descend to warmer levels, but be careful of terrain.

A friend of mine was flying a PA 28 over the mountains and ice started to build. He couldn't climb, and he had to add more and more power to maintain airspeed and altitude. Eventually, the build-up forced the airplane into a slow descent—even on maximum power. He broke out of cloud in a valley with mountains on both sides! He should have turned back immediately or chosen a different track in the first place.

Rime Ice

Rime ice occurs when tiny, supercooled liquid water droplets freeze instantly on contact with a surface the temperature of which is below freezing. Because the droplets are small, the amount of water remaining after the initial freezing is insufficient to cause clear ice. A mixture of tiny ice particles and trapped air results, giving a rough, opaque, crystalline deposit that is fairly brittle and is relatively easy to remove.

Rime ice often forms on leading edges and can affect the aerodynamic qualities of an airfoil or the airflow into the engine. It does not usually cause a significant increase in weight, because it contains much trapped air and accumulates slowly.

The temperature range for the formation of rime ice can be between 0°C and −40°C, but rime ice is most commonly encountered in the range between −10°C and −20°C.

Hoar Frost (White Frost)

Frost occurs when moist air comes in contact with a surface at temperatures less than 0°C. Rather than condensing to form liquid water, the water vapor changes directly into ice and deposits in the form of frost, which is a white crystalline coating that can usually be brushed off. Typical conditions for frost to deposit on the ground or on a parked airplane include a cool, clear night, calm conditions, and high humidity. Frost can form on an airplane when it is parked in temperatures of less than 0°C (this occurs as the result of the freezing of a dew deposit). Frost can also occur in flight when the airplane descends from below-freezing temperatures to warmer moist air, or when climbing through a temperature inversion.

Although frost is not as dangerous as clear ice, it can obscure vision through a cockpit window and affect the lift characteristics of the wings. Frost does not alter the basic aerodynamic shape of the wing like clear ice does, but it can disrupt the smooth airflow over the wing. This causes early separation of the airflow from the upper surface of the wing, resulting in a loss of lift. Frost on the wings is especially dangerous during takeoff, when it may disturb the airflow or increase weight sufficiently to prevent the airplane becoming or remaining airborne.

Icing and Cloud Type

Cumulus Cloud

Cumulus cloud consists predominantly of liquid water droplets at temperatures down to about −23°C, below which either liquid drops or ice crystals may predominate. Newly formed parts of clouds will tend to contain more liquid drops than in mature parts. The risk of airframe icing in cumulus clouds is severe in temperatures between 0°C and −15°C, moderate in temperatures between −15°C and −23°C, and only light in temperatures of less than −23°C. Airframe ice is unlikely in temperatures of less than −40°C.

Since there is a lot of vertical motion in convective clouds, cloud composition may vary considerably at any one level, and the risk of icing may exist throughout a wide altitude band in (and under) cloud. Updrafts will tend to carry the water droplets higher and increase their size. If significant structural icing does occur, it may be necessary to descend into warmer air.

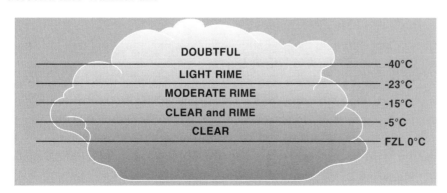

Figure 2-11
Icing in cumulus clouds.

Stratiform Clouds

Stratiform clouds consist entirely or predominantly of liquid water drops down to about −15°C and present a risk of airframe icing. If significant icing is a possibility, it may be advisable to fly at a lower level where the temperature is above 0°C, or at a higher level where the temperature is below −15°C. In certain conditions (e.g. stratiform clouds associated with an active front or orographic uplift), the risk of icing is increased. A continuous, upward motion of air generally means a greater retention of liquid water in the clouds.

Orographic Lift

The extra uplift brought about by mountainous terrain causes clouds to form and enables them to carry additional moisture, thereby increasing the risk of icing. There will be a greater potential for severe clear ice to form, and the freezing level will be lower.

Effect of Cloud Base Temperature

Warm air can hold more moisture than cold air. Therefore, the severity of icing in a convective cloud is liable to be greater in tropical latitudes than temperate ones, and greater in summer than in winter.

High-Level Clouds

High-level clouds, such as cirrus clouds with bases above 20,000 feet, are usually composed of ice crystals that will not freeze onto the airframe. Therefore, the risk of icing is almost nil when flying at very high levels.

Precipitation

Raindrops and drizzle from any sort of cloud will freeze if contact is made with a surface of below 0°C. You therefore need to be cautious when flying in rain at freezing temperatures. This could occur, for instance, when flying in the cool sector underlying the warmer air of a warm front from which rain is falling. Icing can occur in temperatures well above zero, and a pitot (or pitot-static) heater system is provided to prevent this from happening.

Avoiding Ice

In order to avoid ice, make use of forecasts and advisories, and plan your flight to avoid areas of known icing, unless your airplane is equipped with appropriate de-icing (for removal) or anti-icing (for prevention) equipment. Flight into known icing conditions is prohibited in airplanes that do not meet design standards and/or are not certified for such flight.

Preflight in freezing conditions assumes enormous importance. If you can preflight the airplane in the hangar and only take it outside immediately prior to start-up, that's the way to go. If you are flying for pleasure, a cold clear night is great, but consider the risks of ice and snow. Use a separate flashlight for a careful preflight, and save the batteries of your in-flight flashlight.

If you have to remove ice, frost or snow from the airframe before start, check again carefully before takeoff as it may have re-formed. Also, using a hose to wash off the frost or snow may compound the problem by adding moisture which may then turn into clear ice as you taxi in the cold night air.

Wings contaminated by ice will lengthen the takeoff run because of the higher speed needed to become airborne An ice-laden airframe may even be incapable of flight. Ice or frost on the leading edge and upper forward area of the wings is especially dangerous. If taxiing or taking off in below-freezing temperatures, avoid splashing water or slush onto the airframe, since it could freeze onto the structure (if you wash away frost or ice with water, the water may refreeze). Prior to takeoff, check that all airfoils are clean and that there is full and free movement of the controls, flaps, and trim.

It is a good idea to have the pitot heat turned on when flying in rain, even at temperatures greater than 0°C. This helps to keep moisture out of the pitot-static system.

When in flight, ice of any kind on the airframe or propeller or in the carburetor and induction system should be removed immediately. Use de-icing and anti-icing equipment in the manner recommended for your airplane. If the equipment is not coping, change heading or altitude to fly out of icing conditions as quickly as possible. If icing occurs in freezing rain, climbing or descending may take you into warmer air. Consider making a 180° turn (you must notify ATC of any changes to your flight plan).

Carry a little extra airspeed to give an added margin over what could be an increased stall speed, and avoid abrupt maneuvers. Be alert for incorrect readings from the pressure instruments, even if the pitot heat is on.

If possible, avoid cumulus cloud as clear ice may occur at any altitude above the freezing level. If icing occurs while you are in stratus cloud, either descend to warmer air or climb to colder air, say −10°C or less. Act quickly and decisively to prevent the build-up of clear ice becoming so great that it causes significant deterioration in airplane performance. Usually, the safest course of action is to turn back, but this course of action must be taken early.

Even though the temperature is below freezing, flying above cloud layers in clear air will not cause ice to accumulate on the airframe. At the flight planning stage, especially during winter when the freezing level is low, you should check the cloud base, tops, and amount, taking into account actual reports from pilots in flight. In general, you should plan a cruise level that is below or above broken (BKN) cloud, taking the lowest safe altitude into account (you can usually maneuver around scattered (SCT) cloud, but maneuvering around broken cloud is much more difficult). If there is significant cloud, it may be necessary to plan an alternative route over terrain offering a lower lowest safe altitude. This will provide a greater safety margin when attempting to avoid clouds, rain, and icing.

If ice accumulates in flight, appropriate action would include:
- increasing power toward maximum continuous power (to maintain speed and to provide a safety margin over a potentially increased stall speed);
- checking that the pitot heat is on;
- checking that the stall warning and fuel vent heat is on (if installed);
- checking that the windshield heat is on (if installed);
- checking that the propeller de-ice is on (if installed);
- checking that the airframe leading-edge surface de-ice is on (if installed); and
- flying out of the icing conditions.

Flying Out of Icing Conditions

The following is recommended for flying out of icing conditions:
- descending into warmer air above 0°C provided the lowest safe altitude permits this;
- diverting, which may involve a change in track toward lower terrain, or it may mean an 180° turn back out of the localized icing conditions (taking into account that ice accumulation may increase the stall speed significantly, especially in a turn); or
- climbing out of icing conditions, which is usually the least preferred option.

To avoid icing, you should be absolutely certain from reports that climbing to get above cloud will not involve too great a change of level and thus prolonged exposure to more icing (certainly not more than 1,500 feet for a light airplane). Ice will most likely continue to accumulate during a climb, possibly at an even greater rate, because of the slower airspeed and the greater exposure of the under surfaces of the airplane. Also, keep in mind that if the cloud layers are extensive, you may have to descend through more icing conditions with further ice accumulation a possibility.

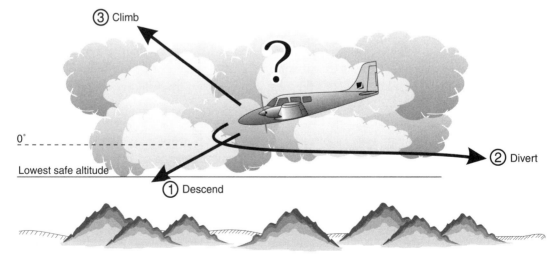

Figure 2-12 Descending, diverting, or climbing to avoid icing conditions.

Fog

Fog is defined as a concentrated suspension of very small water droplets which results in the horizontal visibility at ground level falling to less than ⅝ SM. Fog severely restricts vision near the ground and is the most frequent cause of low visibility at airfields.

At night, the effect of fog is compounded by the generally reduced level of illumination and contrast. Visual navigation may become impossible, and the horizon will be obscured as the aircraft descends into the fog layer. The added visibility of the runway and other lights is also radically affected. The lights, even if they are visible, will be diffused, and judgment of distance and height is less accurate. Also, the clutter of blurred lights may make the runway more difficult to define among other lights. Conversely, river, valley, and sea fog may have little effect during the cruise, as you can see clearly above the inversion layer, and the visibility vertically downwards may not be seriously impaired.

Conditions are likely to be smooth and clear, and the stars will probably shine brightly.

If your night flight is, in fact, a very early morning flight, your destination may be affected by fog. Talk to a pilot with local knowledge. In certain months, morning fogs may preclude early arrivals at some airports.

Formation of Fog

The condensation process that causes fog is associated with the cooling of air by the following means:
- an underlying cold ground or water surface, which causes radiation fog or advection fog;
- the adiabatic cooling of a moist air mass moving up a slope, which causes upslope fog;
- the interaction of two air masses, which causes frontal fog; and
- very cold air overlying a warm water surface, which causes steaming fog.

The smaller the temperature/dewpoint spread and the faster the temperature is falling, the sooner fog will form. An airport with an actual air temperature of +6°C and a dewpoint of +4°C (i.e. a temperature/dewpoint spread of 2°C) early on a calm, clear night is likely to experience fog when the temperature falls 2°C or more from the current +6°C.

Note. A METAR provides both temperature and dewpoint.

Radiation Fog

Radiation fog forms when air is cooled to below its dewpoint by the loss of heat energy through radiation.

Conditions suitable for the formation of radiation fog include:
- cloudless nights that allow the land to lose heat by radiation to the atmosphere and thereby cool, causing the air in contact with the ground to lose heat (leading to a temperature inversion);
- cold land surfaces that promote radiation (radiation fog rarely forms over the sea);

- moist air and a small temperature/dewpoint spread (i.e. a high relative humidity) that only requires a little cooling for the air to reach its dewpoint, causing the water vapor to condense onto small condensation nuclei in the air and form visible water;
- light winds (5–7 knots) that promote the mixing of the air at low level, thereby thickening the fog layer; and
- the presence of condensation nuclei—some types of particles (such as salt) promote fog since they are highly *hygroscopic* (water absorbing).

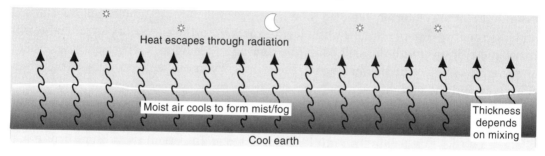

Figure 2-13 Formation of radiation fog.

These conditions are commonly found with an anticyclone or high-pressure system.

Figure 2-14 Wind strength will affect the formation of dew/frost, mist/fog, or stratus cloud.

Air is a very poor conductor of heat, so if the wind is absolutely calm, only the very thin layer of air (1–2 inches thick) in contact with the surface will lose heat to it. This will cause dew or frost to form on the surface itself, rather than cause fog to form in the air above it. If the wind is stronger than about 7 knots, the extra turbulence may cause too much mixing, and instead of radiation fog forming right down to the ground, a layer of stratus cloud may form above the surface.

The temperature of the sea remains fairly constant throughout the year, unlike that of land, which warms and cools quite quickly on a diurnal basis. Radiation fog is therefore much more likely to form over land, which cools more quickly at night, than over the sea.

Dispersal of Radiation Fog

As the surface of the earth begins to warm up after sunrise, the air in contact with it will also warm, causing fog to gradually dissipate. It is common for this to occur by early or mid-morning. The fog may rise to form a low layer of stratus cloud before the sky fully clears. However, if the overnight fog is thick, it may act as a blanket, shutting out the sun and impeding the heating of the earth's surface after sunrise. As a consequence, the air in which the fog exists will not be warmed from below, and the radiation fog may last throughout the day. An increasing wind speed could create sufficient turbulence to drag warmer and drier air down into the fog layer, causing it to dissipate.

Advection Fog (Coastal Fog)

A warm, moist air mass flowing as wind across a significantly colder surface will be cooled from below. If its temperature is reduced to the dewpoint, fog will form. Since the term *advection* refers to the horizontal flow of air, fog formed in this manner is known as *advection fog* and can occur quite suddenly, day or night, if the right conditions exist. Advection fog depends on wind to move a relatively warm and moist air mass over a cooler surface.

Advection fog can be more persistent than radiation fog; for instance, a warm, moist maritime air flow over a cold land surface can lead to advection fog. Unlike radiation fog, the formation of advection fog is not affected by overhead cloud layers, and advection fog can form with or without cloud obscuring the sky. Light to moderate winds will encourage mixing in the lower levels to give a thicker layer of fog, but winds stronger than about 15 knots may cause stratus cloud, rather than fog, to form. Advection fog can persist in much stronger winds than radiation fog.

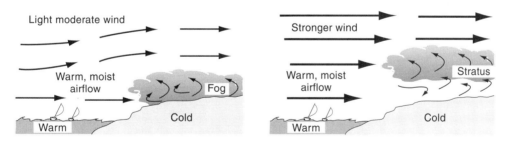

Figure 2-15 Fog or stratus cloud caused by advection.

Sea Fog

Sea fog is advection fog. It may be caused by the following:
- tropical maritime air which moves toward the North or South Poles over a colder ocean or meets a colder air mass; and
- air flow off a warm land surface which moves over a cooler sea, affecting airports in coastal areas.

Dissipation Process

The only way advection fog will dissipate is through a shift in wind direction that changes the source of the air. If the wind is stronger than about 15 knots, the outcome is more likely to be low stratus cloud, which may cause overcast conditions over wide areas.

Upslope Fog

Moist air moving up a slope will cool adiabatically, and if it cools to below its dewpoint, fog will form. This is known as *upslope fog*. It can form whether or not there is cloud above. If the wind stops, the upslope fog will dissipate. Both upslope fog and advection fog depend on wind to exist (but not radiation fog). Upslope fog may be experienced on high ground close to the coast whenever an onshore wind is blowing, but the air needs to be very moist. As a result, upslope fog is more likely to be observed in tropical areas.

Frontal Fog

Frontal fog forms from the interaction of two air masses in one of two ways:
- as cloud that extends down to the surface during the passage of a front, known as *hill fog*, as it mainly forms over hills; or
- as air that becomes saturated by the evaporation of rain, known as *precipitation-induced fog*.

These conditions may develop in cold air ahead of a warm front or an occluded front. The prefrontal fog may be very widespread, giving the impression that the cloud extends from a high level all the way down to the ground. This situation is a killer, as an unwary visual pilot can become trapped in it.

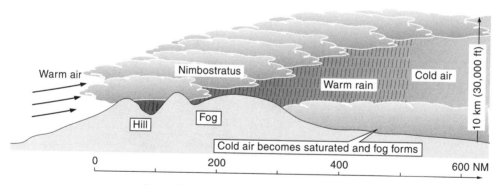

Figure 2-16 Fog associated with a warm front.

Rain or drizzle falling from relatively warm air into cooler air may saturate the air forming precipitation-induced fog, which may be thick, long-lasting, and spread over quite wide areas. Precipitation-induced fog is most likely to be associated with a warm front, but it can also be associated with a slow-moving cold front. This fog moves with the frontal system.

Steaming Fog

Steaming fog can form when cool air blows over a warm, moist surface (a warm sea or wet land), cooling the water vapor which rises from the moist surface to below its dewpoint, thereby causing fog. Low-level turbulence can be present in steaming fog, and there is also a risk of severe icing.

Visibility

Visibility is a measure of how transparent the atmosphere is to the human eye. *Meteorological visibility*, as given in airfield weather reports and forecasts, refers to the greatest distance at which a person of normal sight can correctly identify distant objects. The same criteria apply at night, except that specially selected lights are used to measure visibility.

The minimum visibility, either observed or forecast, is always given in a METAR, SPECI, or TAF. If the minimum visibility covers more than half the airfield, or when visibility is fluctuating rapidly and significant directional variations cannot be given, this is the only visibility information reported.

An accurate assessment of visibility is a factor in determining whether or not an alternate airfield is required. The visibility quoted in an airfield report or forecast is an indication of the real conditions used to determine if the airfield meteorological minima can be met.

Astronomical Times

Sunrise and Sunset

Sunrise occurs when the upper limb of the sun is on the visible horizon and is the first part of the sun to be seen. Sunset occurs when the upper limb of the sun is just disappearing below the visible horizon and is the last part of the sun to be seen.

Twilight

The period of incomplete light (or incomplete darkness) either before sunrise or after sunset is called *twilight*. The period from the start of *morning twilight* until the end of *evening twilight* is called *daylight*. *Morning civil twilight* begins when the center of the sun is six degrees below the celestial horizon. There is usually light enough to see the horizon clearly, yet it is dark enough for bright stars to be visible, depending on atmospheric conditions. Similarly, *evening civil twilight* (and daylight) ends when the center of the sun is six degrees below the celestial horizon.

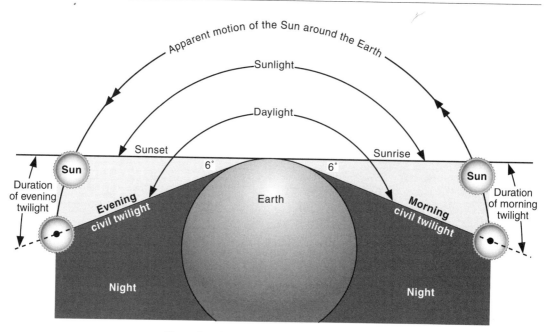

Figure 2-17 Morning and evening civil twilight.

Duration of Twilight

In the tropics, the sun will rise and set at almost 90° to the horizon, which will make the period of twilight quite short and the onset of daylight or night comparatively abrupt. In higher latitudes toward the North and South Poles, the sun will rise and set at a more oblique angle to the horizon, hence the period of twilight will be much longer, and the onset of daylight or darkness will be far more gradual.

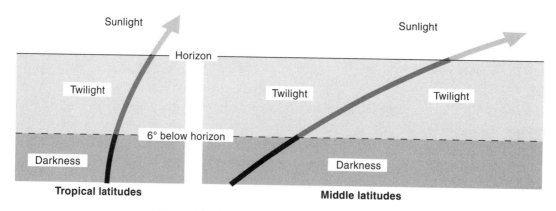

Figure 2-18 Sunrise at tropical and middle latitudes.

During winter inside the Arctic and Antarctic Circles, a period of twilight might occur, but the sun might not actually rise above the horizon at all during the day.

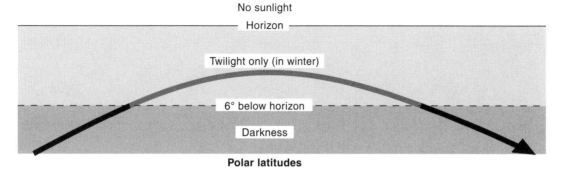

Figure 2-19 Winter twilight in polar latitudes.

Daylight

Factors Affecting the Duration of Daylight
The beginning of daylight (*morning civil twilight*) and the end of daylight (*evening civil twilight*) depend on date and latitude.

Date
In summer, the *beginning of daylight* (BOD) is earlier, and the *end of daylight* (EOD) is later, i.e., daylight hours are longer in summer than in winter.

Latitude
In figure 2-20, places *A*, *B*, and *C* are all on the same meridian of longitude, and therefore all have the same *local mean time* (LMT). However, they are on different latitudes and therefore have different conditions of daylight and darkness:
- at *A*, the sun is well up in the sky, and this location is in full daylight;
- at *B*, the sun is just about to rise (i.e. beginning of daylight); and
- at *C*, the sun has yet to rise—it is therefore still dark (i.e. nighttime).

The shadow line caused by the sun on the earth is called the *terminator*.

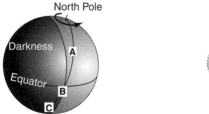

Figure 2-20 Places *A*, *B*, and *C*, although on the same meridian, experience different conditions of daylight and darkness because of different latitudes.

Factors Affecting Daylight Conditions

The time at which the sun rises or sets will depend on the altitude of the observer. For example, to someone on the ground, the sun may appear to have set, but an airplane directly above may still have the sun shining on it. It is possible to be deceived by brightness at altitude, as daylight may have already ended at lower altitudes.

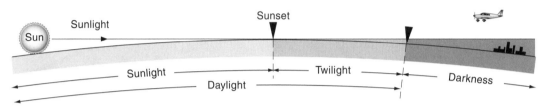

Figure 2-21 An airplane can be in sight of the sun after sunset on the earth below.

High ground to the west of an airfield will also reduce the amount of light as night approaches—remember this when flying.

When the sun is below the horizon, the brightness or darkness of the sky may vary considerably from day to day and place to place, depending on such factors as the amount of cloud cover or other atmospheric variables, including:

- visibility;
- air temperature;
- air pressure;
- humidity; and
- atmospheric refraction.

The amount of high ground between the sun and your position can also affect the brightness of the sky.

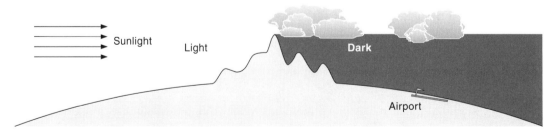

Figure 2-22 Local sunrise and sunset is affected by terrain.

Chapter 3

Human Factors

The Role of the Pilot

The Complete Pilot

We tend to think of piloting an airplane as a physical skill. However, there is more to it—much more. Airplane control—the manipulation of controls to achieve a desired performance—is important, but it is only one element of the pilot's total task. The pilot must assemble information, interpret data and assess its importance, make decisions, act, communicate, correct, and continuously reassess. We call this total process *piloting*.

Decision Making

The essential, fundamental role of the pilot is to make decisions—reliably, safely, and promptly. But fortunately or unfortunately, pilots are only human.

Figure 3-1 The pilot is the data processor.

Emotions in Decisions

Emotion plays a significant, often dominant, role in the decision-making process. We often make decisions on the basis of what we want to happen rather than what is most likely to happen. We can be cautious in our expectations, or we can be ambitious, especially if we have previously pushed boundaries and got away with it.

Decisions also depend on personality and confidence. What chances do we wrongly perceive rather than correctly knowing what the odds really are? Do we err on the positive side or the negative? In terms of safety, the negative is not a bad thing. It is cautious and survival-oriented rather than goal or success oriented—*I made it!* You must learn to make as much of a song-and-dance about sensible, reserved decisions and actions as you would about taking a risk and getting away with it.

Decisions and Stress

Internal Stressors

Indecision causes stress. While you are deciding and are under pressure to decide, your level of stress can become unreasonable. Avoiding a decision also causes stress as you know that, ultimately, the problem will have to be addressed—it will not go away. The solution is to make a decision and go for it. Stress is relieved by action—either fight or flight.

External Stressors

External pressures have a significant effect on decisions. You have human wants, needs, and fears—wanting to please, wanting to impress people, wanting to earn more money or be promoted, needing to be loved, needing to be noticed, needing to be rewarded, fearing criticism or ridicule, fearing job loss, fearing injury… A completely objective decision is made in isolation to such external pressures, and such decisions can often only be made retrospectively—what should have been decided rather than what was decided.

Accident investigations are removed from such external pressures because they do not—cannot—know the pressures under which a particular decision was made. We can rationalize why a pilot should have made a correct decision when we read an accident report—it is obvious to us. Not obvious are the emotional strings attached to that decision. Making correct decisions sometimes takes considerable courage or, to use an old term, *moral fortitude.*

Destination Obsession

Destination obsession (also known as *get-there-itis*) is getting there today at all costs. It seems not to be the result of a conscious, foolish decision but more likely of delaying a decision to turn back and land until it is no longer safe to do so. Illusions and misinterpretation of the seriousness of a deteriorating situation complicate the decision-making process.

The tendency to press on, regardless of the consequences, is particularly insidious as night approaches ("I'll just keep going a little further and a little faster to avoid an unscheduled overnight stop"). The end result is an unplanned and unprepared night sector and an arrival with an over-stressed and over-tired pilot.

This is risky business. Never allow yourself to be placed in this stressful situation where both time and daylight are running out. Take command of the situation and plan for an intermediate stop.

Low Cloud, Pressing On

The problem of pilots pressing on under lowering cloud is well known within the aviation industry, and yet it just does not go away (fatal accidents continue to occur). The solution to the problem is elusive. The decision-making process obviously involves judgment of distances and altitude (distance from cloud and altitude above the terrain). With fewer cues available, those cues that can be read are given greater importance. They appear more pronounced and more compelling in their meaning. They invite greater reliance on what they are telling you. The main effect is to deny a proper and accurate assessment of altitude above terrain and distance from obstacles and cloud, and you have a false appreciation of level attitude.

With restricted forward visibility, your judgment of altitude, attitude, and distance will be so distorted as to be unsafe. You could fly very close to trees or ground without realizing. But by then it is far too late. We have all seen news reports of airplane engine noise low overhead, often for long periods, before the actual impact.

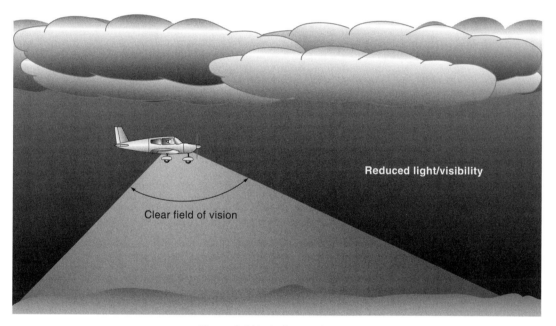

Figure 3-2 Limited cone of vision.

Incredibly *visual meteorological conditions* (VMC) do not require a visual horizon! True, we can estimate the horizontal by perceiving the vertical—by looking down—but this is not always reliable. What if the terrain is not level?

Many airplanes that have crashed into rising terrain under cloud have stalled while under full power. With a limited field of view, there is a tendency to use the ground as a reference for level flight. The closer you get to the ground without a clear attitude reference, the more prone you are to using the vertical as an indication of level flight. In this situation, the climb angle will increase as the slope increases until the inevitable stall.

All of this adds up to the unsurprising conclusion that most, if not all, pilots who continue too far under cloud have no idea how low they are actually flying until they hit something or wind up in the "soup" itself—blind in cloud. In such circumstances, the destination obsession which affected their decision making and distorted their judgment must have been very powerful indeed.

Figure 3-3 Rising terrain—false horizontal.

Personality and Matters of Choice

The idea that some personalities are more prone to taking higher risks than others is not especially controversial. Many of us know people who we would rate as more-likely-than-most to take a higher risk, and a common conviction among such risk takers is "*it won't happen to me.*" The sort or type of person who takes higher risks is usually defined by a *hazardous attitude*.

Five hazardous attitudes that contribute to poor pilot judgment have been identified:

1. Antiauthoritarianism *("don't tell me")*.
2. Impulsivity *("do something quickly")*.
3. Invulnerability *("it won't happen to me")*.
4. Machismo *("I can do it")*.
5. Resignation *("what's the use")*.

Formal Decision-Making Processes

You can learn to make better decisions by itemizing the correct decision-making process as follows:

1. Identify the decision to be made or problem to be solved.
2. Collect relevant information.
3. Generate alternatives.
4. Analyze alternatives.
5. Decide on the most acceptable alternative.
6. Action the alternative.
7. Monitor the outcome: if satisfactory, proceed; if not, repeat steps 2–7.

While this may seem time consuming, these steps give structure and method to the decision-making process and ensures that no conclusions are jumped to. Most airlines use these steps in *crew resource management* (CRM), decision making, and training. It is a valid way to make decisions and to check if your normal decision-making process covers all options.

There is another important element: how much time you have to make a decision. There is a well-known model for decision making based on the mnemonic "DECIDE" which takes reaction time into account:

D Detect a change.
E Estimate the need to react.
C Choose an outcome.
I Identify actions.
D Do the necessary action.
E Evaluate the effect.

However, this model implies that a decision is always a reaction to circumstances, a situation, or a change in events. A better way to make decisions is to anticipate—to be *pro*active rather than *re*active. Have the decision made before it is needed—on standby—as when we practice emergency procedures so we can anticipate a decision point and be able to respond appropriately. Crisis? Ideally, decisions should not be made under duress as in a crisis situation. They should be made under controlled conditions and be stored and ready for use.

A different model for decision making is based on the mnemonic "ACTION:"

A Anticipate and assess the possible scenarios.
C Consider actions and outcomes.
T Time—if available, immediate decision or nominate decision point (go/no-go point), and criteria.
I Implement decision—make a control input, transmission etc.
O Observe the result and correct—fine tune.
N Nominate next milestone, decision point, or potential hazard.

Many problems arise from a lack of decision making or a delayed decision. Decisions are easy to defer. Deferring decisions is only acceptable if a nominated decision point is made and adhered to. By deferring a decision until it is too late, you could be forced into a situation where there is no decision left to make.

Vision

Eyes provide the brain with a visual image of the environment. The basic function of the eyes is to collect light rays reflected from an object, use the lens to focus these rays into an image on a screen (the retina), and convert this image into electrical signals, which are sent via the optic nerve to the brain. This is how we *see*. The brain then matches the image to previously stored data so the object can be recognized (*perceived*). The connection of the optic nerve to the brain is so close and integral, and the importance of the messages sent to the brain is so dominant, that the eyes can almost be considered an extension of the brain.

Structure of the Eye

The main components of the eye are the *cornea* and *lens*, the *retina*, and the *optic nerve*.

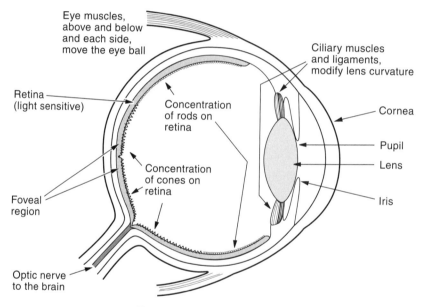

Figure 3-4 Structure of the eye.

Cornea

The cornea is a transparent cap over the lens through which light rays first pass. The surface of the cornea is curved, and light is refracted (bent) as it passes through.

Lens

The lens, like the cornea, is transparent to light, but the curvature of the lens is changed with the ciliary muscles surrounding it, allowing light rays to be focused. The lens provides the fine focus for vision—the greater the curvature, the greater the convergence.

The ability of an eye to change its focus, e.g. from a far object to a near object, is known as *accommodation*. The power of the eyes to accommodate varies, especially with tiredness and age. When a person is fatigued, accommodation diminishes, and blurred images are the result. Also, the lens becomes less flexible and less able to modify its curvature with increasing age. This reduced focusing capability, known as *presbyopia*, is noticed by middle-aged people, and reading glasses are usually necessary.

Iris

Between the cornea and the lens is a colored membrane known as the *iris*. The color of the iris determines the color of the eye. At the center of the iris is a small, round aperture known as the *pupil*. The pupil changes its size to restrict the amount of light entering the lens. In very bright light, the pupil becomes quite small. In very dim conditions, the pupil widens to allow more light to enter.

Retina

The *retina* is a light-sensitive layer located at the back of the eye. It is the screen onto which the lens focuses images, and these images are converted into electrical signals that pass along the optic nerve to the brain. The retina contains two types of light-sensitive (or photosensitive) cells:
- cones; and
- rods.

Cones

Cones are concentrated around the central section of the retina, especially the area of the retina directly opposite the lens, which is known as the *foveal region*. Cones are sensitive to color, details, and distant objects, and they are most effective in daylight and less effective in darkness. They provide the best *visual acuity* (the ability to resolve fine detail). The foveal region is where most objects are focused, and it is this area that provides central color vision in good light conditions. Objects focused on the foveal region in very dim light (as at night) will not stimulate the cones to transmit a message along the optic nerve, so the image will not be seen.

Rods

Rods are concentrated in a band outside the central foveal region and are sensitive to movement but not to detail or color. Rods are effective in both daylight and darkness and are responsible for *peripheral* vision (off-center vision), which helps orientation and night vision. Objects in dim light are therefore most easily noticed when the image falls on the peripheral area of the retina where the rods are concentrated. You can utilize this at night by deliberately looking slightly to the side of an object, rather than directly at it as you would during daylight.

Binocular Vision

Binocular vision describes the process whereby optical information is received and proc-essed from two eyes. To track a moving object with both eyes, they need to move in harmony, and this means coordinated control of the two sets of eye muscles by the brain. In a fatigued person, this coordination sometimes fails, and each eye perceives a different image of the one object, resulting in *double vision*.

When focusing on near objects, the visual axis of each eye will be turned-in slightly; when focusing on distant objects (more than 20 feet away) the visual axes of the eyes will be nearly parallel.

When the eyes are focused on an infinitely distant point, they look straight ahead (i.e. they are parallel). When focusing on nearby objects, distances are estimated by the con-vergence angle of the eye. Light from a particular object, especially a near one, will enter each eye at a slightly different angle, causing different images to be formed by each eye. This is called *stereopsis*. The brain uses these two different images as a means of estimating the distance of nearby objects (the difference in the two images is greater for nearby objects than for distant ones) and the rate of closure.

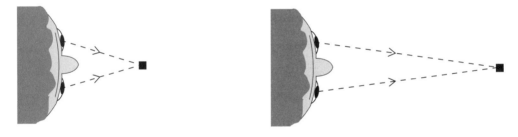

Figure 3-5 Estimating distance—binocular vision.

Absolute distance is judged by *triangulation* (the convergence of sight lines), and this is the prime reason for *binocular vision*. The other reason is to compensate for the *blind spot* in each eye.

The Blind Spot

The blind spot is the small area on the ret-ina where the nerve fibers from the light-sensitive cells (i.e. rods and cones) lead into the optic nerve. At this point, there is no coating of light-sensitive cells, and any light falling here will not register, i.e. it is liter-ally a blind spot. However, it is not possible for an image to fall on the blind spot of both eyes simultaneously because it will be

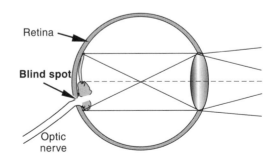

Figure 3-6 The blind spot.

in a different relative position for each eye—when an image falls on the blind spot of one eye and is therefore not registered, the brain will receive a message from the other eye, and the object will still be seen.

You can observe the existence of the blind spot in each eye by viewing the figure below.

Figure 3-7 The blind spot illustrated.

Hold the page at arm's length, cover your right eye, and then with your left eye focus on the airplane on the right. This airplane will be focused on your retina and will be clearly recognizable as a biplane. Stay focused on the biplane and move the page closer. You will notice that the helicopter eventually disappears. Its image has fallen on the position on the retina occupied by the optic nerve, i.e. the *blind spot.*

When scanning the sky, you must be careful that another airplane is not blocked from view by the magnetic compass or some part of the windshield structure. If an airplane is blocked from the view of one eye, you will lose the blind spot protection provided by binocular vision, and you may not see it.

Empty Field Myopia

When you are not trying to focus on any particular object and you are, for instance, just gazing out the windshield into an empty black sky, the natural tendency is for the eyes to focus somewhere in the range of 10 to 30 feet, a condition known as *empty field myopia*, *empty field short-sightedness* or *empty sky myopia*. A pilot flying visually must continually scan the sky for other airplanes and obstacles and then focus on any that are observed. In an empty sky, it requires effort to focus on distant objects, since the eyes tend to focus on a much closer point. Pilots wearing glasses are more susceptible to this phenomenon.

Vision Limitations

Rods and cones are the endings of the optic nerve. As an extension of the brain, they will be affected by anything that affects the brain. With a shortage of oxygen (*hypoxia*) or an excess of alcohol, medication, or other drugs, your sense of sight will suffer. High positive g-loadings, as in strenuous aerobatic maneuvers, will force blood into the lower regions of the body and temporarily starve the brain and eyes of blood, leading to *greyout* (black-and-white tunnel vision) or *blackout* (unconsciousness).

Color Vision

Colors are detected in the central foveal region of the retina by the cone receptors, which are only active in fairly bright light. When these receptors are insensitive to certain shades of light, defective color vision, or *color blindness*, results and usually shows up as a difficulty in distinguishing between red and green. Color blindness may cause problems during night flying, as well as in poor visibility, as red and green navigation lights of other airplanes are used for recognition, and a potential problem may exist with the visual signals from the control tower.

Night Vision

At night, there are some special considerations regarding vision. Your attention during night flying will be both inside and outside the cockpit, and there will be variations in light intensity. It takes the eyes some minutes to adapt to a darker environment (as most of us have experienced when walking into a darkened cinema). The time it takes for the eyes to adapt to varying levels of light depends to a large extent on the contrast between the brightness of light previously experienced and the degree of darkness of the new environment. Conversely, when a darkened environment is suddenly lit (as when the lights are turned on at the end of a movie), the opposite effect takes place. In dim light, the cones become less effective or even totally ineffective, and there is a chemical change in the rods to increase their sensitivity. Thus we adapt more quickly to brightening lights rather than dimming ones. Whereas the cones adjust relatively quickly to variations in light intensity (they take about seven minutes to return to normal), the rods take some 30 minutes to adapt fully to low light.

It is a common misconception that, at night, we are using our night vision in the cockpit or when looking at the runway. When we are looking at something that is well illuminated, we are using normal vision. The night fighter pilots of World War II, for example, did use their night vision. They sat blindfolded in a darkened room before taking off from unlit airfields, and they used red cockpit lighting (and ate carrots) so that they could look for other airplanes or ground features that were not illuminated—there was a blackout (the disadvantage of red cockpit lighting is that red lines or tints on a map, as well as some instrument indications, do not show up). The only equivalent in civil operations is when we are looking for ground features, such as a lake or coastline, or the shadow of hills on a moonlit night. Otherwise, we use normal vision and can set a reasonable level of light within the cockpit (subject to reflections). The correct balance is found when the instruments can be easily read and external lights can be readily detected.

Exposure to glare and bright sunlight should be avoided before night flights—wear sunglasses. If you anticipate being exposed to a bright light (as when an airplane is taxiing on the ramp towards you with its landing light on), close one eye to try to preserve your dark adaptation. Keep the internal lighting to an acceptably low level to minimize reflections and to allow the best transmission of light through the windows. It is the same as other natural processes—the transmission depends on the energy difference from outside to in. More light outside and less light inside provides the best transmission of light through the windows. Even consider wearing a dark colored shirt for night flying as the traditional white pilot's shirt adds considerably to the reflections off the face of the instrument glass. Avoid brilliant lights as they temporarily reduce the sensitivity of the eyes to less well-lit objects. Be especially careful when viewing sunsets and then trying to see down-sun at the darkened earth.

Vision is also affected by reduced oxygen levels, and so at night in a nonpressurized airplane, avoid smoking, and use supplemental oxygen (recommended above 4,000 feet). Note that night vision is susceptible to hypoxia at cabin altitudes above 4,000 feet.

Visual Scanning by Night

Because the central (foveal) region of the retina is not sensitive to low levels of light, this causes an area of reduced visual sensitivity in your central vision. Peripheral vision is more effective. An object at night is more readily visible when you are looking to the side of it by ten or twenty degrees, rather than directly at it. Objects will not be as sharply defined (focused) as in daytime foveal vision.

The most effective way to use your eyes during night flight is to scan small sectors of sky more slowly than you would in daylight. This permits off-center viewing of objects in your peripheral vision and allows you to deliberately focus your perception (mind) a few degrees from your visual center of attention (i.e. direct your eyes at a point but use your peripheral vision to look for objects or lights around it).

Since you may not be able to see another airplane's shape at night, you will have to determine its direction of travel by making use of its visible lighting:

- the flashing or rotating red beacon (usually on the top of the vertical stabilizer);
- the red navigation light on the left wing tip;
- the green navigation light on the right wing tip; and
- a steady white light on the tail.

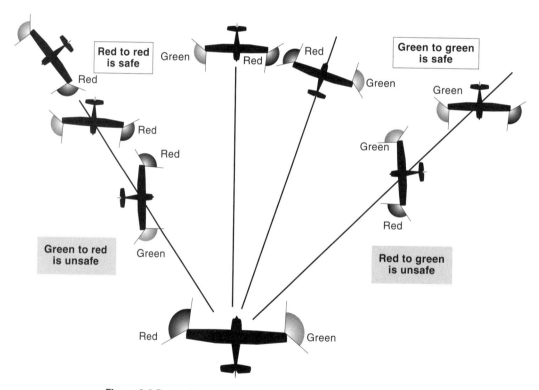

Figure 3-8 Determining airplane direction of travel from airplane lights.

Visual Illusions

Sometimes what we perceive (what we think we see) is not what is actually there, because images sent from the eyes can sometimes be misinterpreted by the brain.

Relative Movement

We are all familiar with the effect that a moving vehicle has on the occupants of an adjacent, stationary one (they think they are moving). The occupants of an airplane moving slowly into a jet bridge may feel that they have sped up if an adjacent airplane is pushed back.

Autokinesis

The visual illusion of *autokinesis*, or self-motion, can occur at night if you stare continuously at a single light against a generally dark background. The light will appear to move, perhaps in an oscillating fashion, after only a few seconds of staring at it, even though it is stationary. You can lose spatial orientation if you use this single light as your sole point of reference. The more you try to concentrate on it, the more it can appear to oscillate, causing you to jerk the controls in an attempt to avoid this moving target.

You can guard against autokinesis at night by maintaining eye movement in normal scanning and by frequently monitoring the flight instruments to ensure correct attitude. Beware also of false horizons at night (see page 59).

False Expectations

From our experiences in the physical world, we build a scale of measurement—size versus distance. For example, if a bus is small in our view, it is perceived as far away, and if a person appears larger than the bus, the person is perceived as closer than the bus. This works well when objects fall within the scale. At night, the estimation of size is almost impossible. Lights on a PA28 may be as bright as those on a B737. The distance between the wing-tip lights does give an indication of size—or is it a smaller airplane closer to you? Passenger cabin window lights give the best indication of airplane size if you can see them. Best of all, change altitude, speed and/or heading so that the lights are not in a constant relative position. Then you are not on a collision course.

Don't rely entirely on vision for separation. Have the transponder on and talk to ATC if you're concerned about possible conflict.

Environmental Perspective (Atmospheric Perspective)

From birth, we develop a mental model whereby indistinct objects are interpreted as distant and clear objects are interpreted as nearby. This is not always so, as atmospheric conditions can alter visibility and can cause pilots to incorrectly judge distances on approach or from mountains (e.g. haze can give a false impression of distance on final).

Judgment of Distance and Angles

The brain often has to make sense of a pattern of lines, and the interpretation may not always be correct. Does a stick bend upwards as it is put into a bucket of water? No, it does not, but it certainly looks as though it does. This is because our brain and eyes assume that light travels in straight lines, which is not always the case as we know from an understanding of *refraction*.

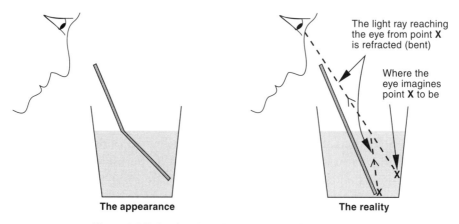

The appearance   **The reality**

Figure 3-9 Refraction alters the appearance of straight lines.

An airplane on approach through heavy rain can sometimes experience a build-up of water on the windshield, and this water can refract light rays entering the cockpit, potentially causing an illusion like the "bent" stick (figure 3-10). Knowledge of this effect can offer some protection to the pilot, as it can also affect the appearance of runway lights during a night approach.

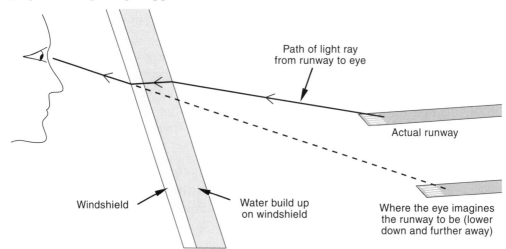

Figure 3-10 Refraction by water on a windshield can alter the pilot's perception of the runway.

False Horizons

Sloping layers of cloud by day, angled lines on the ground, or areas of light by night can sometimes present a pilot with a false horizon. False horizons can be very misleading and can occur with a ragged, lowering cloud base and associated drizzle, rain obscuring the natural horizon, or the combination of stars and city lights.

Crossing large bodies of water at night in single-engine airplanes could be potentially hazardous, not only from the standpoint of landing (ditching) in the water, but also because with little or no lighting the horizon blends with the water, in which case, depth perception and orientation become difficult. During poor visibility conditions over water, the horizon will become obscure, and this may result in a loss of orientation. Even on clear nights, the stars may be reflected on the water surface, which could appear as a continuous array of lights, thus making the horizon impossible to define.

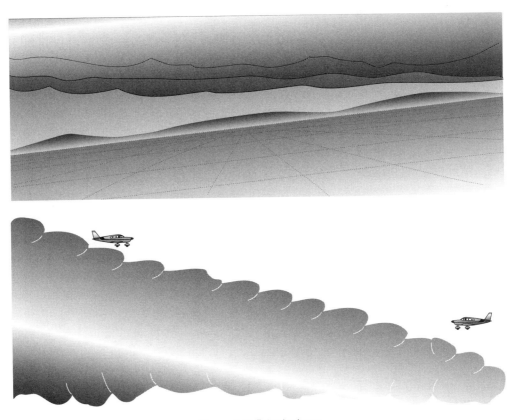

Figure 3-11 False horizons.

Visual Illusions in the Pattern

Visual Estimation of Altitude

Lighted runways, buildings, or other objects may cause illusions to the pilot when seen from different altitudes. At an altitude of 2,000 feet, a group of lights on an object may be seen individually, while at 5,000 feet or higher, the same lights could appear to be one solid light mass. These illusions may become quite acute with altitude changes and if not overcome could present problems in respect to approaches to lighted runways.

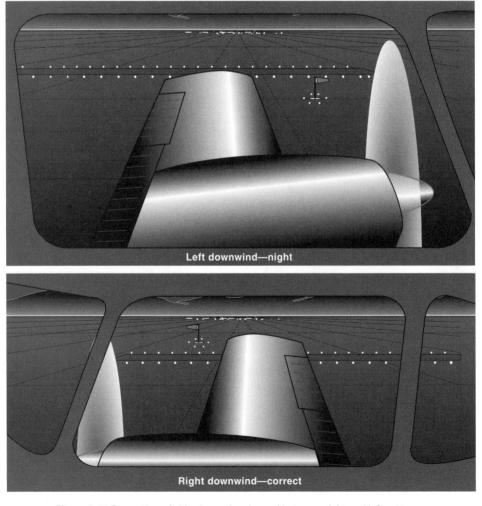

Left downwind—night

Right downwind—correct

Figure 3-12 Perception of altitude can be skewed between right and left patterns.

A pilot flying a right pattern may get the impression that the airplane is higher than normal. This illusion could occur to a pilot who, while flying left patterns, has developed a habit of visually judging pattern altitude and position by relating the position of the runway lights to some feature of the airplane, such as a particular position in a side window. While such a rule of thumb may work satisfactorily for the more typical left patterns, it could lead a pilot to descend lower to achieve the same picture when making right patterns. Like most habits, such a practice could happen unconsciously.

Visual Illusions on Approach

Runway Slope

Most runways are of standard width and are on flat ground. On every approach, you should try to achieve the same flight path angle to the horizontal. Your eyes will become accustomed to this; by keeping your view of the runway through the windshield in a standard perspective, you will be able to make consistently good approaches along an acceptable approach slope. However, when approaching a sloping runway, the perspective will be different.

A runway that slopes upward will look longer, and you will feel that you are high on slope, when in fact you are right on slope. The tendency will be for you to go lower or make a shallower approach.

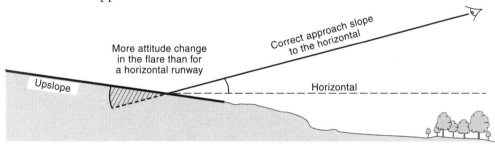

Figure 3-13 Upsloping runway.

A runway that slopes downward will look shorter, and you will feel that you are low on slope when in fact you are on the correct path. The tendency will be for you to go higher and make a steeper approach.

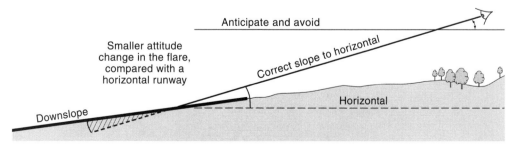

Figure 3-14 Downsloping runway.

If you know the runway slope, you can make allowances for being high or low on approach in your visual estimation (refer to figure 3-15).

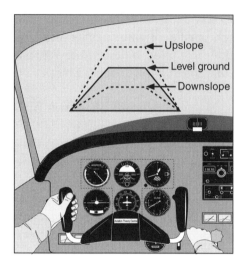

Figure 3-15
Runway slope can alter
perception of approach path.

Runway Size

A runway that is wider than usual will appear to be closer than it really is. Conversely, a runway that is narrower than usual will appear to be further away than it really is. Because of the angle at which you view it peripherally in the final stages of the approach and landing, a wide runway will also cause an illusion of being too low, and you may flare and hold-off too high as a result. This may lead to "dropping in" for a heavy landing. A narrow runway will cause an illusion of being too high, and you may delay the flare and make contact with the runway earlier (and harder) than expected.

If you know that the runway is wider or narrower than your regular airfield, you can allow for this in your visual judgment of flare height.

Figure 3-16
Runway width can alter
perception of distance
to a runway.

Night Approach

At night, a powered approach is preferred. Power gives the pilot more precise control, a lower rate of descent, and a shallower approach path. The approach to the aim point should be stabilized as early as possible (constant airspeed, path, attitude, thrust, and configuration). Use all the available aids, such as the runway lighting and a *visual approach slope indicator* (VASI). If the runway edge lighting is the only aid, correct tracking and slope is achieved when the runway perspective is the same as in daylight. On centerline, the runway will appear symmetrical. Guidance on achieving the correct approach slope is obtained from the apparent spacing between the runway edge lights and the distance of the aim point below the horizon.

If the airplane is low, the runway lights will appear to be closer together or closing. If the airplane is above slope, the runway lights will appear to be further apart and separating. VASI will provide correct indications, but the perspective provided by runway edge lighting may be misleading because of runway slope or width.

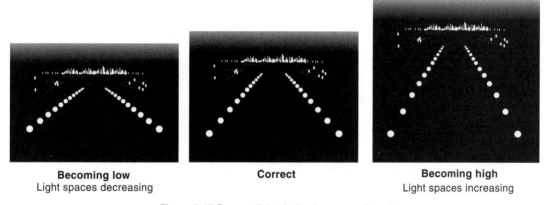

| **Becoming low** | **Correct** | **Becoming high** |
| Light spaces decreasing | | Light spaces increasing |

Figure 3-17 Runway lights indicating approach path.

Black-Hole Approach

Flying an approach to a runway with no other visible references can often be difficult. This can occur when approaching a runway on a dark night where the only visible lights are the runway edge lights, with no town or street lights or any other indication of the nature of the surrounding terrain. This is known as a *black-hole approach*. Alternatively, there could be city lights in the area beyond the airfield but no visual cues near the threshold. Black-hole approaches also occur on islands, at remote desert airfields, and on approaches to runways that are surrounded by water.

Black-hole approach   **Approach with good ground reference**

Figure 3-18 Lack of visible ground references at night can cause difficulty in flying an approach.

The tendency is to think that you are higher than you actually are, resulting in an urge to descend and fly a shallower approach—to sink into the abyss, the black hole.

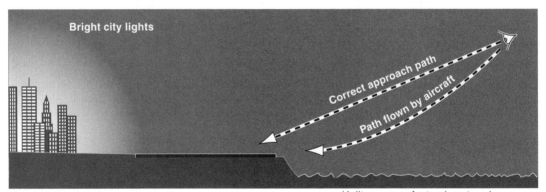

Unlit ocean or featureless terrain

Figure 3-19 Black-hole approach causes a shallower approach.

The worst black-hole problem of all occurs at remote airfields on dark nights (say under cloud) where there is no other light source or any ground texture, and autokinesis might generate an impression of movement when there is none. Rely on the instruments, not your eyes, to maintain horizontal and vertical navigation plots.

If VASI is not available, cross-check the vertical speed indicator to ensure that the rate of descent is proportional to the approach speed (V_{REF}). As a guide, the rate of descent should be close to 5 times the ground speed for a 3° approach.

Obscured approach   Normal perspective

Figure 3-20 Lack of ground references causes a difficult approach.

A similar situation to a black-hole approach, known as a *white-out approach*, arises in conditions where the ground is covered with snow, making it featureless. The lack of a visual horizon and details around the runway threshold make depth and slope perception much more difficult.

Summary

A variety of atmospheric and terrain conditions can produce visual illusions on approach. When you encounter these situations, you can anticipate and compensate for them.

Situation	Illusion	Result	
Upslope runway or terrain	Greater height	Lower approach	Shallower
Narrower than usual runway	Greater height	Lower approach	
Featureless terrain	Greater height	Lower approach	
Rain on the windshield	Greater height	Lower approach	
Haze	Greater height	Lower approach	
Downslope runway or terrain	Less height	Higher approach	Steeper
Wider than usual runway	Less height	Higher approach	
Bright runway and approach lights	Less distance	Higher approach	

Table 3-1 Summary of visual illusions on approach.

Focal Point

The most common visual illusion is not so much an illusion as distorted judgment. It is based on a familiar phenomenon known as the *inappropriate habit*. Let us say you routinely fly into a given airfield. You assess that you have reached the base turn position on the basis of a *that-looks-about-right* distance assessment.

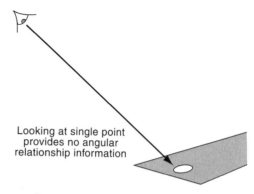

Looking at single point provides no angular relationship information

Figure 3-21 Single point lock-on problem.

The distance that looks about right during the day in clear conditions will be greatly different from the distance that looks about right at night, or under heavy overcast conditions, or through light rain. The basis of your distance judgment is stored knowledge accumulated over the number of approaches you have made along that same track to that same runway. The vast majority of your flights through these points will have been made in good weather—clear skies, bright sunlight, and great visibility—not in gloom or darkness.

If you are aware of potential illusions, you can make corrections to your perceptions. If your image of a given runway at a given airfield is based on past experience in clear conditions, the tendency will be for you to fly closer to that same runway until you can match that image in terms of contrast or intensity when conditions are poor. You will need to use discipline and other reference features to get the right distance.

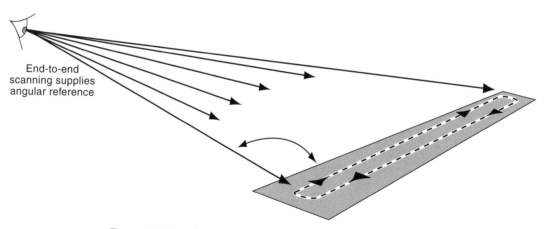

End-to-end scanning supplies angular reference

Figure 3-22 Conscious scan for centerline and glide slope information.

The problem is compounded when you are preparing to turn final. In good weather, you have a complete picture of the runway centerline, which is necessary to position on final. When visibility is limited, you lack one of the two points needed to project the line, i.e. the extended centerline. Instead, you concentrate on the nearest, clearest point on the runway—the threshold (where else?). This is the *focal point*. Your cue to turn final is activated by your judgment of an angular relationship with the runway, which, in this situation, you cannot determine.

If you are focusing solely on the one point in poor visibility, you simply cannot establish the correct lead angle at which to commence the final turn. You need to force yourself to scan, looking at each end of the runway in turn to imagine a centerline.

The problem is worse at night, and the need for a formal scan is greater. There is a similar problem with looking at the runway on approach. Focusing unconsciously or otherwise on one point denies you glide slope information. You will only get that through a conscious scan.

Another important reference is any light on the horizon which is on or close to the projected runway centerline. It puts everything into perspective.

Hearing and Balance

The ears provide two senses—hearing and balance. Hearing allows us to perceive sounds and to interpret them. Balance allows us to interpret which way is up and whether or not we are accelerating. After vision, balance is the next most important sense for a pilot.

Balance and acceleration signals from the balance mechanism in the inner ear pass to the brain as electrical signals for interpretation. In the case of an airborne pilot, the interpretation is sometimes tricky, since the brain is accustomed to upright and slow-moving states on the earth's surface.

Structure of the Ear

The ear is comprised of three parts: the outer ear, the middle ear, and the inner ear.

Outer Ear

The outer section of the ears includes:
- the external ear (known as the *pinna* or *auricle*), which is used to gather sound signals;
- the *outer canal* through which pressure waves pass; and
- the *eardrum*, which is caused to vibrate in harmony with pressure waves.

Any obstruction to the outer canal, such as earplugs or an excess of wax, can prevent sound pressure waves from reaching the eardrum. Similarly, a padded cover over the external ear can prevent sound waves entering the ear (unless the cover is a headset that blocks external noise but has a small speaker for radio and interphone messages).

Middle Ear

The middle ear is an air-filled cavity containing three small bones, known as *ossicles*. The ossicles are forced to move by the vibrating eardrum, converting the pressure-wave energy into mechanical energy of motion. The ossicles are arranged like a series of levers to increase the effect of the initial movement. This energy then passes on to the *cochlea* in the inner ear. Together with the eardrum, the ossicles constitute the *conductive tissue*.

The air in the middle ear is maintained at ambient atmospheric pressure via the *Eustachian tube*, which connects the interior of the middle ear to the nasal passage. There should be no leakage of air across the eardrum, and there should be easy passage of air through the Eustachian tube to equalize pressure, e.g. when climbing or descending. The passage of air is sometimes hindered by mucus, swelling, or inflammation (e.g. when a person has a cold) and can lead to serious consequences. Interference to the movement of the three small ossicles or their joints will reduce or distort sound signals. This can be caused by ear infections, damage to the bones or joints, or a blocked ear with air trapped inside (*barotitis*).

The region of the middle ear provides sensations of movement and balance, and for this reason middle ear infections can affect the sense of balance. Furthermore, disturbed signals from middle-ear sensors can lead to a feeling of nausea. In extreme cases, this can result in *vertigo*—the total loss of balance with massive and disturbing disorientation.

At night, there is less likelihood of a clear horizon. Our best visual reference is compromised, and we are even more vulnerable to inner-ear sensations and misinterpretations.

Inner Ear

The innermost section of the ear contains three very important pieces of apparatus:
- the *cochlea*;
- the *vestibular apparatus*; and
- the *otolithic organs*.

The cochlea converts the mechanical energy from the ossicles into electrical signals that then travel via the auditory nerve to the brain for interpretation.

The vestibular apparatus consists of three fluid-filled *semicircular canals* that sense angular acceleration. There is a cluster of small hairs at the base of each semicircular canal. These sensing hairs sit at the base of each canal in a chamber known as the *cupula*. Interaction between the hairs and the fluid in the canals provides sensations of movement.

In the same region are the *otolithic organs*, which detect linear (fore and aft, up and down) acceleration or deceleration. The otolithic organs are co-located with, but separate from, the vestibular apparatus. Fluid in the cochlea is moved by the mechanical energy from the ossicles, and this causes a wavy movement of small hairs protruding into the fluid. The movement is converted into electrical signals at the bottom of each hair, and these signals are sent along the auditory nerve to the brain.

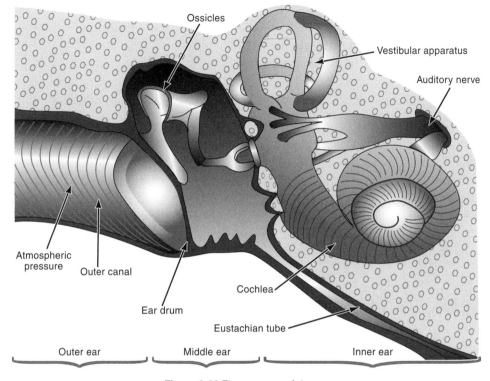

Figure 3-23 The structure of the ear.

Balance

The sense of balance makes it possible for us to remain upright. The most powerful reference for balance is the visual channel. If you can see, you can tell whether or not you are vertical (providing there is a vertical or horizontal reference). If you close your eyes, your orientation is not so easy to gauge—you can confirm this by standing on one leg with your eyes closed. The secondary sensing mechanisms (i.e. other than vision) are those from which your brain might be sent orientation messages. The secondary signals are feeble compared to visual cues and really only supplement visual perception. In other words, they can only make sense in partnership with the vastly more powerful visual picture. These sensory mechanisms are designed for three-dimensional orientation but not three-dimensional motion or acceleration. If you have no visual horizon, these other sensors will supply fall-back information, albeit information that is not reliable.

In the absence of a powerful visual cue, your system will crave orientation signals and accord them equal weight. The secondary sensing mechanisms will be perceived as very strong, but they will always be misleading. You cannot rely on any of them, and you must *never* use them to judge your flight path. However, you can guard against their influence by knowing what they will try to tell you and by becoming familiar with their illusory signals.

Spatial Orientation

Orientation is the ability to determine your position and alignment in space. It is usually achieved by a combination of three senses:

- vision, which is the most powerful sense;
- balance, which is the *vestibular* sense (gravity, acceleration, and angular acceleration); and
- bodily feel, or what pilots call *seat of the pants*, which is the *proprioceptive* sense.

The brain uses all available information to assemble a picture, but if there are conflicting signals, vision is given first priority. In most situations, vision, balance, and bodily feel reinforce each other. However, this is not always the case in flight, where each of these senses can sometimes have its messages misinterpreted by the brain. When you are denied external vision and flying is solely by reference to the instruments, a range of false sensations can be perceived. Not knowing your attitude in relation to the horizon (i.e. which way is up) is called *spatial disorientation*. When you are denied external vision, you need to rely totally on your flight instruments and scan to check that they agree with each other.

Human Balance Mechanism

The balance mechanism, the vestibular apparatus, is designed to keep us upright—i.e. vertical and balanced while standing or moving. In the absence of visual references, the inner ear can sense what is perceived as verticality by sensing *tilt* (angle) and sensing *tilting* (motion—backward/forward or left/right). The angle of tilt is sensed by the otoliths (a pendulous mass which senses gravity), and the tilting motion is sensed by the fluid-filled semicircular canals.

Sensing Gravity (Verticality)

Gravity is detected by the sensory hairs in the *otolithic organs*, which can be thought of as membranous sacs filled with gelatinous material. The outer membranes of the sacs are studded with small crystals of calcium carbonate called *otoliths*, hence the term otolithic organs.

The otolithic organs have a resting position when the head is upright. The brain interprets the message sent from the small hairs at this time as *up*, i.e. a direct downward force of 1g. If the head is tilted to one side or forward or backward, the otoliths move under the force of gravity and take up a new position. This bends the hairs, which then send a different signal to the brain.

The otolithic organs can detect the direction of g-forces, but they cannot distinguish the origin of the forces—e.g. whether it is the force of gravity or a centripetal force pulling you into a coordinated turn. We must remember that the body is designed for fairly slow motion on the face of the earth with a consistent 1g force of gravity exerted on it and not for the three-dimensional forces experienced in flight (or zero g for that matter). In a turn, the otolithic organs will recognize a false vertical.

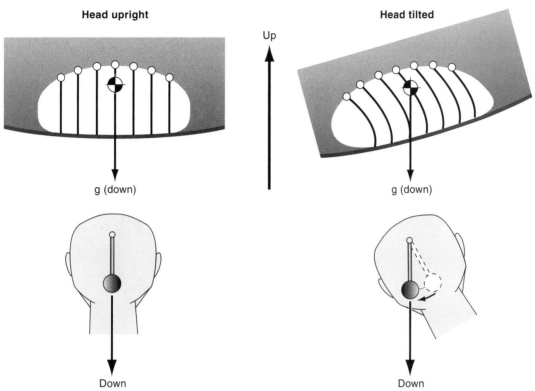

Figure 3-24 Gravity sensed by the otholithic organs.

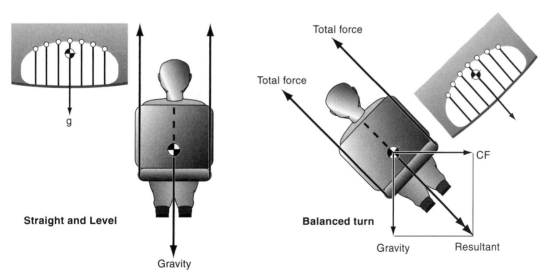

Figure 3-25 In a turn, the otholithic organs will recognize a false vertical.

Sensing Linear Acceleration

When our bodies are tilted or accelerated, we naturally lean to avoid falling over. In the absence of a visual reference, the body cannot discriminate between tilting and accelerating, and our corrections may not be appropriate.

Sensing Angular Movement

The three *semicircular canals* of the inner ear (part of the vestibular apparatus) contain fluid. The canals are at right angles to each other (they are orthogonal) like the pitch, roll, and yaw planes of an airplane. Therefore, they can detect angular acceleration (the change in the rate of rotational speed) in pitch, roll, and yaw.

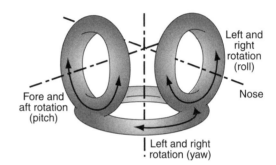

Figure 3-26
The semicircular canals.

The *cupula* is a saddle-shaped chamber at the base of each canal as depicted in figure 3-27. It has a cluster of fine hairs that protrudes into the fluid. Movement in the fluid is sensed by these hairs. Nerve endings at the base of the hairs send corresponding signals to the brain for interpretation (perception).

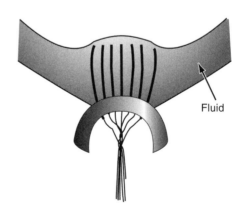

Figure 3-27
The cupula.

The semicircular canals are *not* designed to detect linear changes in motion *or* linear acceleration because the upper and lower volumes of fluid are self-cancelling. For exam-

72

ple, if the fluid at the top of the semicircular canal tries to move counterclockwise around the canal because of an acceleration forward, the fluid at the bottom will try to move around clockwise to the same degree. The net effect is there will be no relative movement of the fluid, and the sensory hairs of the cupula will remain straight.

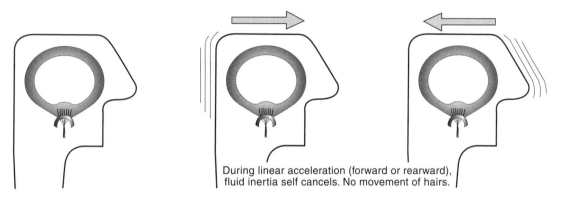

During linear acceleration (forward or rearward), fluid inertia self cancels. No movement of hairs.

Figure 3-28 Linear acceleration not detected by the semicircular canals.

The vestibular apparatus senses angular acceleration by recognizing changes in rotary motion because of the lag of the viscous fluid. During angular acceleration, the relevant semicircular canal moves around a mass of fluid that lags. This lag in the fluid bends the sensory hairs, and this sends a signal to the brain that the head is rolling, yawing, or pitching (three dimensions—three channels—three canals).

When the rate of roll steadies, i.e. there is no more angular acceleration, the fluid will catch up with the surface of the semicircular canals, and the sensory hairs of the cupula will straighten. For this reason, you will detect an entry to a roll but not its continuing steady state. Similarly, you will sense an opposite acceleration as you stop a roll (decelerate) at the required bank angle.

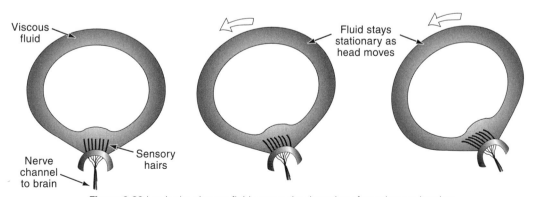

Viscous fluid

Fluid stays stationary as head moves

Nerve channel to brain

Sensory hairs

Figure 3-29 Lag in the viscous fluid causes the detection of angular acceleration.

Normal Sensations Associated with a Level Turn

As is the case with any stimulus or sensation, there is a threshold below which movement will not be detected. For example, you will sense a sharp change in roll rate, but you may not sense a gentle change. In reality, you do not necessarily detect the angular acceleration that commences a roll as a rolling sensation. You will feel the entry into a roll as a rolling sensation if the roll is sharp enough. Similarly, you will sense the rotary deceleration that stops a roll at the selected bank angle. You may also sense rolling signals from adjustments to the control input while amending either roll rate or angle of bank. However, in many flight regimes, your control inputs will be so gentle that you will not detect any rolling sensation at all. In such situations, the potential for confusion is serious.

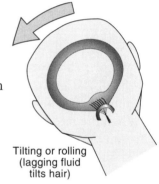

There is angular acceleration when you enter a turn. Angular deceleration occurs when you stop the roll at the desired bank angle. The roll onset (build-up) period is very brief—from when you move the controls until the roll is underway—a fraction of a second. The stop-the-roll period is also brief. Nonetheless, these accelerate–decelerate stages may or may not be sensed by your semicircular canals, depending on whether or not the accelerate–decelerate stages exceed the minimum threshold of detection. Very low rates will not be noticed, but you will sense the commencement and cessation of a sharp roll.

When a roll is induced, the pilot's head also rolls, and the little sensing hairs are immediately bent by the fluid lagging in the canal. The fluid flows relative to the canal, but it is actually the canal (your head) that is moving around the fluid. Owing to inertia, the fluid temporarily lags until friction with the walls of the canal brings it "up to speed."

Tilting or rolling (lagging fluid tilts hair)

The hesitant fluid in the canal bends the hairs. Electrical signals go to the brain: "*We are rolling to the left.*" When a steady roll is underway, the fluid will catch up, and the hairs will return to their normal, erect position. The sensation of rolling thus dissipates, although the roll could be continuing. However, as most roll movements are brief, the dissipation of the roll sensation is not significant. The roll will usually be stopped before the hairs are neutralized.

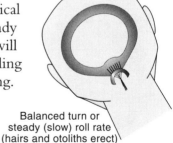

Balanced turn or steady (slow) roll rate (hairs and otoliths erect)

Figure 3-30 (Right) The semicircular canals will sense the angular acceleration (deceleration) of a roll into (out of) a turn, provided it is large enough.

In a sustained turn, there is no rolling motion. The bank angle is constant. The resultant of the force of gravity and centrifugal force aligns the otholithic organs to a *false* vertical. In a perfectly coordinated 60° banked turn, you will experience a 2g force exerted by the seat on your body at an angle of 60° to the vertical. With no visual reference, you will feel as if you are still sitting upright with respect to the external forces. You cannot know if you are level or in a banked turn. You need visual cues to confirm your actual attitude.

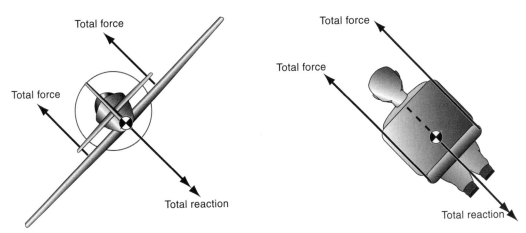

Figure 3-31 No rolling motion in a coordinated turn.

It's just like a carousel.

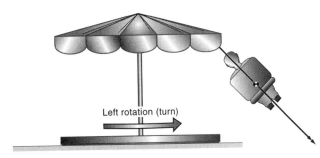

Figure 3-32 Ooo weee!

Sensations in Turning Flight

In a coordinated turn, a full glass of water on top of the instrument panel will remain unspilled—the fluid will remain level with respect to the glass (figure 3-33, page 76). It is as if the weight of the fluid is acting through the normal axis of the airplane. It is. The apparent weight is the result of gravity and centrifugal reaction.

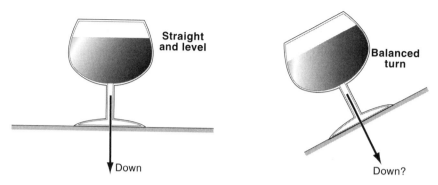

Figure 3-33 Water will not be spilled in a coordinated turn.

Your body will also sense up and down as acting in that same axis. In the example illustrated in figure 3-31, the start-roll and stop-roll movements are sensed, and the latter cancels out the residue of the former. There will no longer be any rolling sensation. Nor is there any other sensation source apart from the *seat of the pants*. In other words, when you are established in a turn, you will feel as if you are in straight-and-level flight, and that feeling will be the same regardless of the bank angle (although load factor will vary).

Disorientation and Illusions
The Leans

When you combine a false sense of vertical with the sensation of rolling, the brain can become very confused. This condition is known as *the leans*. The leans can interfere profoundly with your mental equilibrium, but only if you let them.

Consider the situation in which an entry into a right turn is very gentle. The entry is not sensed by the semicircular canals, but the stop-roll deceleration is detected. The end result is quite discomforting. The gentle onset of roll into the turn would not be perceived, and no sensation would be available during the steady-state roll. If stop-roll control movements are made briskly, the angular deceleration that stops the roll and establishes the bank angle would be felt—strongly. However, it would be felt as a roll to the left. As there would be no cancelling sensation available, the sensation of rolling—continuous rolling—would persist, though it would slowly dissipate as the fluid stops moving and the sensory hairs stand up straight again.

In entering this right turn, the only sensation perceived would be the stop-roll angular deceleration. The signal sent to the brain would be read as roll to the left. With no corresponding cancelling sensation, it would be a sensation of continuous rolling. If you then roll out of the turn and the roll-out is briskly commenced (i.e. enough to be detected), you would then experience the sensation that the left-roll movement has become faster.

Perception of rapid roll rates can quickly produce strong sensations of disorientation. You can also get the leans during turn entry or exit. That is:

- you might be wings level and yet absolutely convinced you are rolling into or established in a turn; or
- equally, you might be in a turn and yet be certain that your wings are level.

We have seen that slow rates of roll (or movement around the other two axes) will not be detected. However, brisk control inputs will induce sensations, and the brisker the input, the stronger the sensation.

A common leans scenario would be when you slowly let a wing drop then suddenly notice the wing-low condition. To counter this, you spontaneously—and rapidly—roll to wings level (and perhaps be looking down at a map or over your shoulder for the runway after a night takeoff). You then feel a strong rolling sensation—the leans.

Nose-Up Pitch Illusion of Linear Acceleration

When you tilt your head back or lean backward, the otoliths act as tiny weights which cause the sacs of the otolithic organs to slump in the same direction. The corresponding sensor-hair movement tells your brain that your vertical axis is now inclined rearward. The same sensation is caused by linear acceleration. Under acceleration, the sacs lag behind, and the sensor-hair movement sends a message to your brain that you are tilting backward. This sensation is known as the *somatogravic illusion* (from *somato* meaning "originating in the body" and *gravic* meaning "sense of gravity").

Pilots experience somatogravic illusion as the sensation of the nose rising during acceleration (*nose-up pitch illusion*), and the greater the acceleration, the stronger the feeling. Obviously, this is not a problem when there are clear visual cues, but it can have very serious consequences when there are few or no cues, as on a dark night. In these conditions, forward acceleration through takeoff and then to climb speed will be sensed as backward tilt, i.e. as a higher nose-attitude and pitch-up than actually exist, and there will be a temptation to lower the nose—which if carried through could prove fatal.

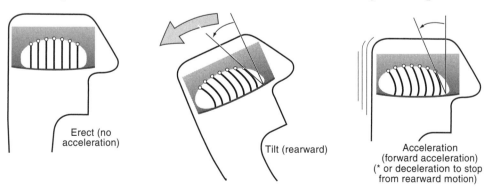

Erect (no acceleration)

Tilt (rearward)

Acceleration (forward acceleration) (* or deceleration to stop from rearward motion)

Figure 3-34 Nose-up pitch illusion because of linear acceleration.

Nose-Down Pitch Illusion of Linear Deceleration

There is a converse to the somatogravic illusion, but it not as serious as it is less likely to happen near the ground. Deceleration in flight is sensed as tilting forward (figure 3-35).

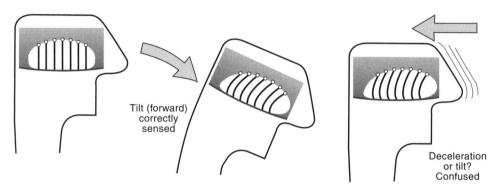

Figure 3-35 Nose-down pitch illusion because of linear deceleration.

This *nose-down pitch illusion* is particularly noticeable in higher performance airplanes when thrust is reduced and speed brakes are extended. If the airplane is already descending, the deceleration will be sensed as a steepening descent. Again, if there is a clear visual reference, the sensation is hardly noticeable. However, if there is no visual reference, the illusion will be more powerful. *Fly attitude.*

Night Factors

We are already familiar with the insidious and debilitating effects on the pilot of:
- motion sickness;
- stress (due to noise, heat, time, and peer group pressures);
- fatigue (due to tiredness, stress, circadian rhythms, and phases);
- reduced sensory arousal (there are less things to see and do at night, and we are therefore sleepy, drowsy, and dreamy);
- hypoxia (noticeable at lower altitudes at night);
- smoking; and
- carbon monoxide.

If the individual pilot is in circumstances in which several of these effects come into play, there is a serious risk of loss of awareness, loss of command, and loss of control.

A night flight should come as a result of planning and preparation. An unplanned extension of a long day into a night arrival is an unwise alternative. It is better to stop and rest and start afresh and early the next day—even before sunrise. It's a great time to be airborne.

Part 2

Night Flight Rules and Requirements

Chapter 4

Night Flight Rules and Requirements

Although flying in visual conditions, there may not be a visual horizon during night operations; therefore, night flight requires a greater understanding of the operation and utilization of flight instruments and navigation aids. There are also additional considerations with regard to regulations and procedures to be taken into account when planning a flight at night.

What Is Night?

Night is defined in the Aeronautical Information Manual (AIM) as the period between the end of evening civil twilight and the beginning of morning civil twilight. Day is the period of time from the beginning of morning civil twilight to the end of evening civil twilight. Civil twilight is a twenty-minute period just after sunset and just before sunrise.

How To Determine if a Pilot Is Suitable To Fly Night VFR

Student Pilots

Student pilots may not operate an aircraft in solo flight at night unless they have received:
- flight training at night on night flying procedures that include takeoffs, approaches, landings, and go-arounds at night at the airport where the solo flight will be conducted;
- navigation training at night in the vicinity of the airport where the solo flight will be conducted; and
- an endorsement in the student's logbook for the specific make and model of aircraft to be flown for night solo flight by an authorized instructor who gave the training within the ninety-day period preceding the date of the flight.

Solo flight operations at night require flight or surface visibility of at least 5 statute miles, and the flight must be made with visual reference to the surface.

Recreational Pilots

A recreational pilot may not fly solo or act as pilot in command (PIC) between sunset and sunrise, when the flight or surface visibility is less than 3 statute miles, or without visual reference to the surface. For the purpose of obtaining additional certificates or ratings while under the supervision of an authorized instructor, a recreational pilot may fly as the sole occupant of any aircraft between sunset and sunrise, provided the flight or surface visibility is at least 5 statute miles.

Private Pilots

A person who applies for an unrestricted private-pilot certificate must receive and log ground and flight training from an authorized instructor on night operations. These operations must include night flying, takeoffs, landings, VFR navigation, and emergency operations, including simulated aircraft and equipment malfunctions. Being able to identify and use a suitable landing area in the dark is an important and necessary skill. Aeronautical experience must include:

- 3 hours of night-flight training (dual, solo, or a combination thereof);
- one cross-country flight of over 100 nautical miles total distance; and
- 10 takeoffs and 10 landings to a full stop (with each landing involving a flight in the traffic pattern) at an airport.

An applicant who does not meet these requirements will be issued a private pilot certificate with the limitation "NIGHT FLYING PROHIBITED." This restriction may be removed if the certificate holder later demonstrates that these requirements have been met.

Commercial Pilots

A person applying for a commercial pilot certificate must log at least five hours of solo night flight in VFR conditions, with 10 takeoffs and 10 landings (with each landing involving a flight in the traffic pattern) at an airport with an operating control tower. The commercial-pilot applicant must also fly one cross-country flight of at least two hours in night VFR conditions, consisting of a total straight-line distance of more than 100 nautical miles from the original point of departure.

An applicant who does not meet these requirements will be issued a commercial pilot certificate with the limitation "NIGHT FLYING PROHIBITED." This restriction may be removed if the certificate holder presents to an examiner a logbook or training record endorsement from an authorized instructor verifying that these requirements have been accomplished.

Airline Transport Pilots

A person applying for an airline transport pilot (ATP) certificate must have at least 100 hours of night flight time.

Carrying Passengers

No person may act as PIC of an aircraft carrying passengers during the period beginning one hour after sunset and ending one hour before sunrise, unless within the preceding 90 days:

- that person has made at least three takeoffs and three landings to a full stop during the period beginning one hour after sunset and ending one hour before sunrise;
- that person acted as sole manipulator of the flight controls; and
- the required takeoffs and landings were performed in an aircraft of the same category, class, and type (if a type rating is required).

Airplane Equipment

Airplane equipment must be considered carefully in determining whether or not an airplane is suitable to be flown at night. Considerations include external and internal lighting, cockpit instrumentation, emergency equipment, radio equipment, and NAVAID equipment. The following outlines the minimum equipment that must be serviceable for night flight.

Day Requirements

The following lists the requirements for day VFR flight:
- an airspeed indicator;
- an altimeter;
- a magnetic direction indicator;
- a tachometer for each engine;
- an oil pressure gauge for each engine using a pressure system;
- a temperature gauge for each liquid-cooled engine;
- an oil temperature gauge for each air-cooled engine;
- a manifold pressure gauge for each altitude engine;
- a fuel gauge indicating the quantity of fuel in each tank;
- a landing gear position indicator, if the aircraft has a retractable landing gear;
- an approved aviation red or aviation white anti-collision light system (for airplanes manufactured after 1996);
- flotation gear (for aircraft operated for hire over water and beyond power-off gliding distance from shore);
- safety belts and shoulder harnesses; and
- an emergency locator transmitter (ELT).

Night Requirements

For VFR flight at night, all of the day requirements must be met. In addition, the airplane must have:
- approved position lights;
- an approved aviation red or aviation white anti-collision light system (regardless of when they were manufactured);
- one electrical landing light (if the aircraft is operated for hire);
- an adequate source of electrical energy for all installed electrical and radio equipment;
- one spare set of fuses, or three spare fuses of each kind required, that are accessible to the pilot in flight; and
- enough fuel to fly to the first point of intended landing and, assuming normal cruising speed, to fly after that for at least 45 minutes.

Although not required by regulations, it is recommended that supplemental oxygen be used by pilots at altitudes exceeding 5,000 feet MSL during night operations.

Pilot Equipment

Before beginning a night flight, carefully consider the equipment that should be readily available during the flight (putting the flashlight on a lanyard and hanging it around your neck will ensure it doesn't roll under your seat). At least one reliable flashlight is recommended as standard equipment on all night flights. A flashlight with a bulb-switching mechanism that can be used to select white or red light is preferable; use the white light while performing the preflight visual inspection of the airplane, and use the red light when performing cockpit operations. Since the red light is non-glaring, it will not impair night vision. A word of caution: if a red light is used for reading an aeronautical chart, the red features of the chart will not show up. Remember to place a spare set of batteries in your flight kit.

Aeronautical charts are essential for night cross-country flight, and if the intended course is near the edge of the chart, the adjacent chart should also be available. The lights of cities and towns can be seen from surprising distances at night, and if this adjacent chart is not available to identify those landmarks, confusion could result. Regardless of the equipment used, organization in the cockpit helps to ease the burden on the pilot and to enhance safety.

Aircraft Lighting

No person may operate between sunset and sunrise unless their airplane has lighted position and anti-collision lights. The anti-collision lights need not be lighted when the PIC determines that, because of operating conditions, it would be in the interest of safety to turn the lights off. Also, no person may park or move an aircraft in—or in dangerous proximity to—a night-flight operations area of an airport unless the aircraft is clearly illuminated, has lighted position lights, or is in an area that is marked by obstruction lights.

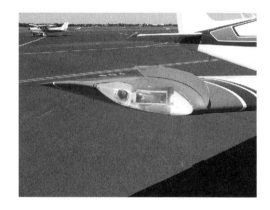

Figure 4-1
Right-hand wing tip with strobe light and green navigation light (red on left wing tip).

For collision avoidance, a pilot must know where each colored light is located on an aircraft (refer to figure 3-8, page 56). By knowing the position lights, you can determine an aircraft's direction of flight. For example, if a pilot observes a steady red light and a flashing red light ahead at the same altitude, the other aircraft is crossing to the left. A steady white and a flashing red light indicates that the other aircraft is headed away from the observer, and steady red and green lights at the same altitude as the observer indicates that the other aircraft is approaching head-on (see figure 3-8 on page 56).

The FAA has a voluntary pilot safety program, "Operation Lights On," to enhance the see-and-avoid concept. Pilots are encouraged to turn on their landing lights during takeoff; i.e., either after takeoff clearance has been received or when beginning the takeoff roll. Pilots are further encouraged to turn on their landing lights when operating below 10,000 feet, day or night, especially when operating within 10 miles of any airport or in conditions of reduced visibility, and in areas where flocks of birds may be expected (e.g., coastal areas, lake areas, or around refuse dumps). Although turning on aircraft lights does enhance the see-and-avoid concept, pilots should not become complacent about keeping a sharp lookout for other aircraft.

Interior lights should be kept low at night.

Part 135 Night Operations

No person may operate an aircraft carrying passengers under Part 135 VFR at night unless the aircraft is equipped with:

Figure 4-2
Rotating beacon on top of fin
(also a white light at rear of fuselage).

- a gyroscopic rate-of-turn indicator;
- a slip skid indicator;
- a gyroscopic bank-and-pitch indicator;
- a gyroscopic direction indicator;
- a generator or generators able to supply all probable combinations of continuous in-flight electrical loads for required equipment and for recharging the battery;
- an anti-collision light system;
- instrument lights to make all instruments, switches, and gauges easily readable, the direct rays of which are shielded from the pilot's eyes;
- a flashlight having at least two size D-cells or equivalent;
- two-way radio communications equipment able, at least in flight, to transmit to—and receive from—ground facilities 25 miles away; and
- navigational equipment able to receive signals from the ground facilities to be used.

Weather Requirements

When planning for a night flight, you must consider cloud, visibility, wind, and other general weather conditions, as you would for a flight by day. However, it is much more difficult to see cloud at night, so you must make a careful study of the weather in conjunction with the terrain in the vicinity of your planned flight.

No person may operate an aircraft under VFR when the flight visibility is less—or at a distance from clouds that is less—than that prescribed for the corresponding altitude and class of airspace in the following table:

Airspace	Flight Visibility	Distance From Clouds
Class A	Not applicable	Not applicable
Class B	3 statute miles	Clear of clouds
Class C, Class D, Class E less than 10,000 feet MSL	3 statute miles	500 feet below, 1,000 feet above, 2,000 feet horizontal
Class E at or above 10,000 feet MSL	5 statute miles	1,000 feet below, 1,000 feet above, 1 statute miles horizontal
Class G 1,200 feet or less AGL, Day	1 statute mile	Clear of clouds
Class G 1,200 feet or less AGL, Night	3 statute miles	500 feet below, 1,000 feet above, 2,000 feet horizontal
Class G more than 1,200 feet AGL but less than 10,000 feet MSL, Day	1 statute mile	500 feet below, 1,000 feet above, 2,000 feet horizontal
Class G more than 1,200 feet AGL but less than 10,000 feet MSL, Night	3 statute miles	500 feet below, 1,000 feet above, 2,000 feet horizontal
Class G more than 1,200 feet AGL and at or above 10,000 feet MSL	5 statute miles	1,000 feet below, 1,000 feet above, 1 statute mile horizontal

Table 4-1 VMC criteria.

Notwithstanding the provisions of table 4-1, the following operations may be conducted in Class G airspace below 1,200 feet AGL—when the visibility is less than three statute miles but not less than one statute mile during night hours, an airplane may be operated clear of clouds if operated in an airport traffic pattern within one-half mile of the runway.

Special VFR operations may only be conducted if the person being granted the ATC clearance is instrument-rated and the airplane is equipped for an IFR flight. A Special VFR clearance is not an option at night for the VFR-only pilot.

Airport Lighting

The lighting systems used for airports, runways, obstructions, and other visual aids at night are important aspects of night flying. Lighted airports located away from congested areas can be identified readily at night by the lights outlining the runways. Airports located near or within large cities are often difficult to identify in the maze of lights. It is important not only to know the exact location of an airport relative to the city, but also to be able to identify that airport by the characteristics of its lighting pattern.

Prior to a night flight, and particularly a cross-country night flight, check the availability and status of lighting systems at the destination airport. This information can be found on aeronautical charts and in the Airport/Facility Directory. The status of each facility can be determined by reviewing pertinent Notices to Airmen (NOTAMs).

Airfield Lighting Aids

Airfield lighting aids that may be installed on an airport include the following.

Approach Light System (ALS)

The approach light system is an airport lighting facility which provides visual guidance to landing aircraft by radiating light beams in a directional pattern by which the pilot aligns the aircraft with the extended centerline of the runway on the final approach for landing. Condenser-discharge sequential flashing lights or sequenced flashing lights may be installed in conjunction with the ALS at some airports. Types of approach light systems are outlined below.

ALSF-1

ALSF-1 is an approach light system (ALS) with sequenced flashing lights in ILS Cat-I configuration.

ALSF-2

ALSF-2 is an approach light system (ALS) with sequenced flashing lights in ILS Cat-II configuration. The ALSF-2 may operate as an SSALR when weather conditions permit.

SSALF

SSALF is a simplified short approach light (SSAL) system with sequenced flashing lights.

SSALR

SSALR is a simplified short approach light (SSAL) system with runway alignment indicator lights.

MALSF

MALSF is a medium intensity approach light system (MALS) with sequenced flashing lights.

MALSR

MALSR is a medium intensity approach light system (MALS) with runway alignment indicator lights.

LDIN

The lead-in light system consists of one or more series of flashing lights installed at or near ground level that provides positive visual guidance along an approach path, either curving or straight, where special problems exist with hazardous terrain, obstructions, or noise abatement procedures.

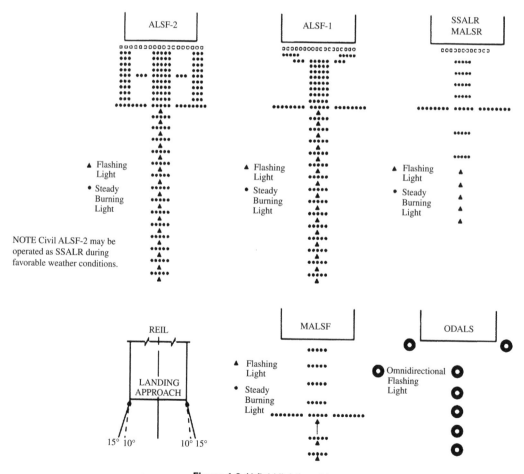

Figure 4-3 Airfield lighting aids.

RAIL

Runway alignment indicator lights consist of sequenced flashing lights which are installed only in combination with other light systems.

ODALS

The omnidirectional approach lighting system consists of seven omnidirectional flashing lights located in the approach area of a non-precision runway. Five lights are located on the runway centerline extended, with the first light located 300 feet from the threshold and extending at equal intervals up to 1,500 feet from the threshold. The other two lights are located, with one on each side of the runway threshold, at a lateral distance of 40 feet from the runway edge, or 75 feet from the runway edge when installed on a runway equipped with a visual approach slope indicator (VASI) system.

Runway Lights

Runway Edge Lights

Runway edge lights are used to outline the runway at night or during periods of low visibility. For the most part, runway edge lights are white (while taxiways are outlined in blue omnidirectional lights) and may be high-, medium-, or low-intensity.

Touchdown Zone Lighting

Touchdown zone lighting consists of two rows of transverse light bars located symmetrically about the runway centerline, normally at one-hundred-foot intervals. The basic system extends 3,000 feet along the runway.

Runway Centerline Lighting

Runway centerline lighting consists of flush centerline lights spaced at fifty-foot intervals, beginning 75 feet from the landing threshold and extending to within 75 feet of the opposite end of the runway.

Threshold Lights

Threshold lights are fixed green lights arranged symmetrically left and right of the runway centerline, identifying the runway threshold.

Runway End Identifier Lights (REIL)

Runway end identifier lights consist of two synchronized flashing lights, one on each side of the runway threshold, which provide rapid and positive identification of the approach end of a particular runway.

Boundary Lights

Boundary lights consist of lights defining the perimeter of an airport or landing area.

Taxiway Edge Lights

Taxiway edge lights are used to outline the edges of taxiways during periods of darkness or restricted visibility conditions. These fixtures emit blue light (while runway edge lights are usually white) that outlines the usable limits of taxi paths. At most major airports, these lights have variable intensity settings and may be adjusted at pilot request or when deemed necessary by the controller.

Summary

The VFR pilot needs to be familiar with the basic lighting of runways and taxiways. The basic runway lighting system consists of two straight parallel lines of runway edge lights defining the lateral limits of the runway. These lights are aviation white, although aviation yellow may be substituted for a distance of 2,000 feet from the far end of the runway to indicate a caution zone. At some airports, the intensity of the runway edge lights can be adjusted to satisfy the individual needs of the pilot. The length limits of the runway are defined by straight lines of lights across the runway ends. At some airports, the runway threshold lights are aviation green, and the runway end lights are aviation red. At many airports, the taxiways are also lighted.

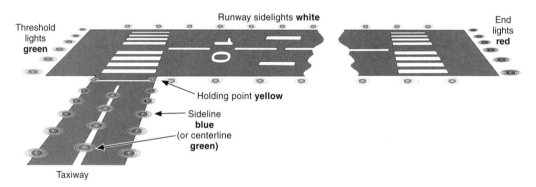

Figure 4-4 "Simple" runway lights a VFR pilot can expect.

Beacons

At night, the location of an airport can be determined by the presence of an airport rotating beacon light. The colors and color combinations that denote airport type are given in table 4-2 (page 91).

Note. Green alone or amber alone is used only in connection with a white-and-green or white-and-amber beacon display, respectively.

A civil-lighted land airport beacon will show alternating white and green flashes. A military airfield will be identified by dual-peaked (two quick) white flashes between green flashes.

Lights	Indication
White and green	Lighted land airport
Green alone	Lighted land airport
White and yellow	Lighted water airport
Yellow alone	Lighted water airport
Green, Yellow, White	Lighted heliport

Table 4-2
Airport rotating
beacon lights.

Obstruction Lights

Obstructions are marked/lighted in order to warn pilots during daytime and nighttime conditions. Obstructions may be marked/lighted in any of the following combinations.

Aviation Red Obstruction Lights

These are flashing aviation red beacons (20 to 40 flashes per minute) and steady burning aviation red lights during nighttime operations. Aviation orange and white paint is used for daytime marking.

Medium Intensity Flashing White Obstruction Lights

Medium intensity flashing white obstruction lights may be used during daytime and twilight with automatically selected reduced intensity for nighttime operation. When this system is used on structures 500 feet AGL or less in height, other methods of marking and lighting the structure may be omitted. Aviation orange and white paint is always required for daytime marking on structures exceeding 500 feet AGL. This system is not normally installed on structures less than 200 feet AGL.

High Intensity White Obstruction Lights

These are flashing high intensity white lights used during daytime with reduced intensity for twilight and nighttime operation. When this type system is used, the marking of structures with red obstruction lights and aviation orange and white paint may be omitted.

Dual Lighting

This is a combination of flashing aviation red beacons and steady burning aviation red lights for nighttime operation, and flashing high intensity white lights for daytime operation. Aviation orange and white paint may be omitted.

Catenary Lighting

Lighted markers are available for increased night conspicuousness of high-voltage (69KV or higher) transmission line catenary wires. Lighted markers provide conspicuousness both day and night.

Obstruction Light Indications

High intensity flashing white lights are being used to identify some supporting structures of overhead transmission lines located across rivers, chasms, gorges, and so on. These lights flash in a middle, top, lower light sequence at approximately 60 flashes per minute. The top light is normally installed near the top of the supporting structure, while the lower light indicates the approximate lower portion of the wire span. The lights are beamed towards the companion structure and identify the area of the wire span.

High intensity flashing white lights are also employed to identify tall structures, such as chimneys and towers, as obstructions to air navigation. The lights provide a 360-degree coverage about the structure at 40 flashes per minute and consist of from one to seven levels of lights, depending upon the height of the structure. Where more than one level is used, the vertical banks flash simultaneously.

Pilot Activated Lighting

Pilot activated lighting (PAL) is a system through which the pilot can turn on a lighting system using a coded VHF carrier wave. The availability of the system will be noted on the chart and in the A/FD for the airport concerned.

Radio control of lighting provides airborne control of lights by keying the aircraft's microphone. The control system is responsive to 7, 5, or 3 microphone clicks:

- keying the microphone 7 times within 5 seconds will turn the lighting to its highest intensity;
- keying the microphone 5 times in 5 seconds will set the lights to medium intensity; and
- low intensity is set by keying the microphone 3 times in 5 seconds.

Wind Direction Indicator Lighting

A wind cone, wind sock, or wind tee may be installed near the operational runway to indicate wind direction. The large end of the wind cone or sock points into the wind as does the cross bar of the wind tee. The tetrahedron, wind cone, wind sock, or wind tee may be located in the center of the segmented circle and may be lit for night operations.

Visual Approach Slope Indicator (VASI)

The visual approach slope indicator (VASI) is a lighting system arranged so as to provide visual–descent guidance information during approach to a runway. The lights are visible for up to 5 miles during the day and up to 20 miles or more at night. The VASI glide path provides obstruction clearance, while lateral guidance is provided by the runway or runway lights. When operating to an airport with an operating control tower, the pilot of an airplane approaching to land on a runway served by a VASI is required to maintain an altitude at or above the glide slope until a lower altitude is necessary for landing.

Most VASI installations consist of two bars, near and far, which provide one visual glide path. On final approach flying toward the runway of intended landing, if the pilot sees both bars as red, the aircraft is below the glide path. Maintaining altitude, the pilot will see the near bar turn pink and then white, while the far bar remains red, indicating the glide path is being intercepted. If the aircraft is above the glide path, the pilot will see both near and far bars as white.

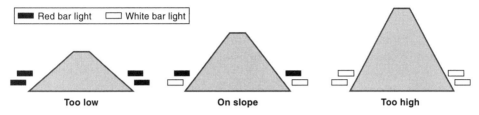

Figure 4-5 Two-bar VASI.

Tri-color visual approach slope indicators normally consist of a single light unit projecting a three-color visual approach path. The below-glide path indication is red, the above glide path indication is amber, and the on glide path indication is green.

Figure 4-6 Three-bar VASI.

Pulsating VASIs normally consist of a single light unit projecting a two-color visual approach path. The below glide path indication is normally red or pulsating red, and the above glide path indication is normally pulsating white. The on glide path indication is usually steady white.

Precision Approach Path Indicator (PAPI)

The precision approach path indicator (PAPI) uses a single row of lights. Four white lights means "too high," while one red light and three white lights means "slightly high." These systems have an effective visual range of about 5 miles during the day and up to 20 miles at night.

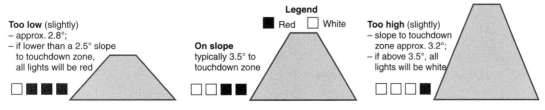

Figure 4-7 PAPI.

Altitudes

When flying VFR at night, in addition to the altitude appropriate for the direction of flight, pilots should maintain an altitude which is at or above the minimum en route altitude (MEA) as shown on charts. This is especially true in mountainous terrain, where there is usually very little ground reference. Do not depend on your eyes alone to avoid rising unlit terrain, or even lighted obstructions such as TV towers. Keep in mind that flying higher at night will increase your vision to aid pilotage, increase NAVAID reception, and increase your gliding distance (but keep in mind weather and oxygen requirements).

Night IFR Operations

Precision approach radar (PAR) facilities operated by the FAA and the military services at some joint-use (civil and military) and military installations monitor aircraft on instrument approaches and issue radar advisories to the pilot when weather is below VFR minimums (1,000 and 3), at night, or when requested by a pilot. This service is provided only when the PAR final approach course coincides with the final approach of the navigational aid and only during the operational hours of the PAR. The radar advisories serve only as a secondary aid, since the pilot has selected the navigational aid as the primary aid for the approach.

When landmarks used for navigation are not visible at night, the approach will be annotated "PROCEDURE NOT AUTHORIZED AT NIGHT."

Part 3

Piloting Technique

Chapter 5

Instrument Flight Technique

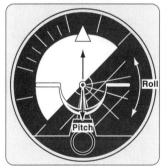

Pilots should practice and acquire competency in straight-and-level flight, climbs, descents, level turns, climbing turns, descending turns, and steep turns—all with reference to the instruments. This is because night operations are essentially VFR-on-instruments flight. Recovery from unusual attitudes should also be practiced, but only on dual flights with a flight instructor. In addition, practice these maneuvers with all the cockpit lights turned off. This blackout training is necessary—if you experience an electrical or instrument light failure, you will have to read the instruments by flashlight.

Figure 5-1 Pitch remains pitch.

Flight Control versus Flight Performance

There is a direct relationship between the techniques used for instrument flight and those used for visual attitude flight as required for day or night operations. In visual flight, an attitude is set with reference to the visual horizon together with a power setting (and/or configuration change) to achieve a desired performance. The performance of the airplane is assessed by scanning performance instruments, and then, if necessary, small adjustments to attitude and/or power are made to ensure the desired performance is eventually attained. When this happy state of affairs has been reached, the airplane is trimmed to ensure the selected attitude can be maintained with minimum effort on our part.

In instrument flight, the visual horizon is substituted for an *artificial* horizon displayed on the attitude indicator. The other important consideration is the need to develop a more systematic approach to instrument scanning. Also, it is fair to say that instrument flight requires a more measured and precise technique for airplane control and trimming, i.e. a slower and softer touch is required.

Pitch and bank attitudes are established using the attitude indicator. However, it is important to appreciate that relatively large pitch-attitude changes against the natural horizon are represented in miniature on the instrument. For instance, for a typical light airplane in straight-and-level flight at cruise speed, the wing bars of the miniature airplane might appear against the horizon line of the instrument. At low airspeed, the wings might be one or even two bar widths above the horizon, whereas for a climb attitude in the same airplane, the wing bars of the miniature airplane might be positioned two or three bar widths above it (or 10° if the AI has degree increments). In a turn, the wing bars of the miniature airplane will bank along with the real airplane, while the horizon line will remain horizontal. The center dot of the miniature airplane represents the position of the nose relative to the horizon.

Instrument Scanning

Simple Scans

Each scan is simple, starting at the attitude indicator and radiating out to the relevant instrument before returning again to the attitude indicator. The attitude indicator is the focal point of each scan because it is the primary control instrument. The scan pattern radiates out from and back to the attitude indicator no matter what the airplane is doing. This is called a *selective radial scan*.

The airplane can be accurately and comfortably flown without any external visual reference, provided the instruments are scanned efficiently and the pilot controls the airplane adequately in response to the information provided by the instruments.

The attitude indicator (AI) shows pitch attitude and bank angle directly, but it does not show yaw. Coordination information is obtained simply by moving the eyes from the attitude indicator diagonally down left to the turn coordinator to confirm that the ball is centered. The eyes must then return to the attitude indicator (figure 5-2).

Heading is obtained from the heading indicator (HI) or magnetic compass. From the attitude indicator, the eyes move straight down to the heading indicator to check heading before returning to the attitude indicator (figure 5-3).

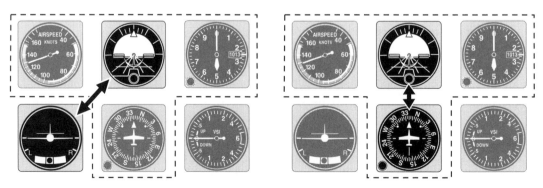

Figure 5-2 A simple scan for coordination.   **Figure 5-3** A simple scan for heading.

Airspeed is easily checked by moving the eyes left from the attitude indicator to the airspeed indicator (ASI) before returning to the attitude indicator (figure 5-4).

To read altitude, the eyes move from the attitude indicator to the right where the altimeter (ALT) is located before moving back to the attitude indicator (figure 5-5).

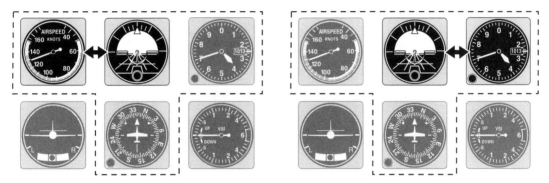

Figure 5-4 A simple scan for airspeed.   **Figure 5-5** A simple scan for altitude.

The rate of climb or descent is read by moving the eyes from the attitude indicator diagonally down to the right to the vertical speed indicator (VSI) before returning to the attitude indicator (figure 5-6).

Turn rate is read from the turn coordinator (TC) when the bank angle is established. The normal rate of turn in instrument flying is 3°/second, known as a *standard-rate turn* or a *rate-one turn*. Turn rate is clearly marked on the turn coordinator or turn indicator (figure 5-7).

Figure 5-6 A simple scan for vertical speed information.   **Figure 5-7** A simple scan for turn rate.

Control Instruments and Performance Instruments

The combination of attitude plus thrust determines the flight path of the airplane. Accordingly, the two instruments that indicate these—the attitude indicator and the power indicator—are known as the *control instruments*. The pilot has no direct indication of flight path, so the *performance instruments* are used to deduce the flight path from altitude, airspeed, rate of climb and descent, heading, or heading change indications. Further, the airplane's position is shown by the *navigation instruments*.

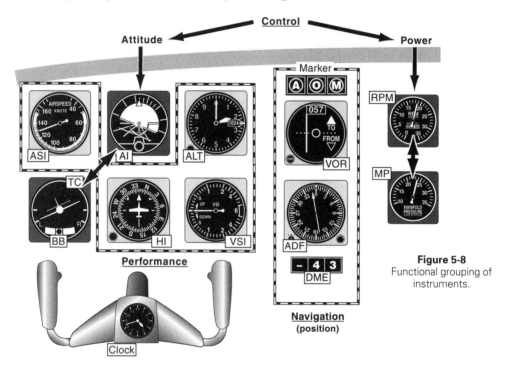

Figure 5-8
Functional grouping of instruments.

The performance instruments show the flight path (as a result of the power and attitude selected) in terms of:

• altitude on the altimeter and vertical speed indicator;
• direction on the heading indicator and turn coordinator; and
• airspeed on the airspeed indicator.

Configuration also determines performance (e.g. speed brakes, flaps position, cowl flaps, and landing gear). For simplicity, a constant configuration is assumed when we say attitude and power determines performance.

Because continuous reference to power is not necessary, the power indicator is situated slightly away from the main group of flight instruments. It can be scanned easily, but it is not in the main field of view. It can also be set by the tone of the engine and by throttle position (a very important cue).

Selective Radial Scan

As stated, the technique of looking from the attitude indicator to a selected instrument and returning to the attitude indicator is known as a *selective radial scan*.

Selective radial scanning is a logical process, and it ensures that a high priority is given to the attitude indicator—the primary control instrument—as well as the performance instruments relevant to the maneuver being undertaken, i.e. when climbing, turning, or descending, the relevant performance instruments take their appropriate place. Let us examine how radial scanning works in practice.

Figure 5-9 Selective radial scan.

Climbing

With climb power selected, the estimated climb attitude is set on the attitude indicator, and when stabilized, the airplane is trimmed. Reference is then made to the airspeed indicator to confirm that the selected pitch attitude is correct. (The airspeed indicator provides the pilot with the needed feedback.) If the airspeed indicator shows an airspeed that has stabilized but is too low, a lower pitch attitude on the attitude indicator is required (perhaps a half bar width lower). A few seconds must then be allowed for the airspeed to settle.

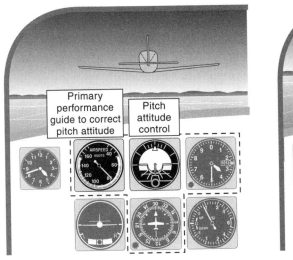
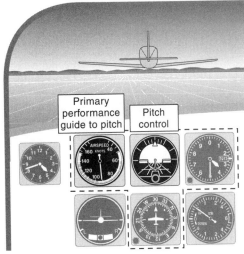

Figure 5-10 The airspeed indicator is the primary instrument in the climb to confirm and adjust pitch attitude.

Leveling Off and Cruising

When approaching cruise altitude, attention is paid to the altimeter to ensure that the airplane levels off at the desired altitude as pitch attitude is lowered on the attitude indicator.

The altimeter and vertical speed indicator are guides to the rate of change of attitude. When straight and level, any minor deviations from altitude can be corrected with small changes in pitch attitude. Therefore, the altimeter is the primary performance guide for pitch attitude in the cruise. It is supported by the vertical speed indicator.

If climb power is maintained after leveling at cruise altitude, the airplane will accelerate. At the desired cruise speed, the power should be set to the appropriate cruise power setting.

Heading is monitored with reference to the heading indicator, and any deviations are corrected with small, coordinated heading changes. The heading indicator will show whether or not coordinated, wings-level flight is being conducted. The heading indicator is therefore the primary feedback to maintaining wings level.

The coordination ball is used to cancel sideslip.

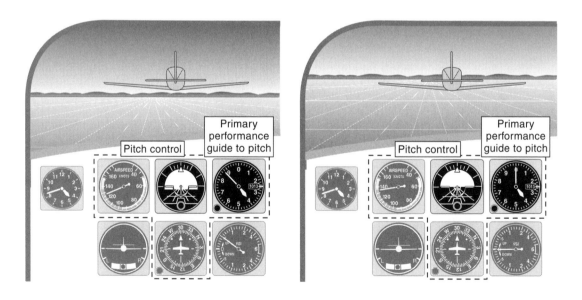

Figure 5-11 The altimeter is the primary instrument in the cruise to confirm and adjust pitch attitude.

Use the Logical Scan for Each Maneuver

Starting with the attitude indicator, scan the performance instruments which are relevant to the maneuver being conducted. To determine whether or not the pitch attitude selected on the attitude indicator is correct, primary pitch information is obtained from the altimeter during cruise flight, and it is obtained from the airspeed indicator during climbs and descents. There is no need to memorize particular scan patterns, as they will develop naturally.

Avoid fixating on one instrument, as this will certainly cause a breakdown in the scan pattern. Fixation on any one instrument may also result in delayed recognition of flight path and/or airspeed deviations. For example, fixation on the heading indicator might enable a given heading to be maintained, but this would be of no use in the detection of altitude and airspeed errors—errors that would be seen (and corrected) if the altimeter, vertical speed indicator, and airspeed indicator were scanned. Keep the eyes moving, but return to the attitude indicator.

Occasionally, other items in the cockpit will need to be attended to—for example, setting engine and mixture controls following a power change, checking fuel, suction, and electrical system gauges, reading instrument approach charts, tuning radios or filling in a flight log. Consequently, the scan will need to be expanded, and attention will need to be momentarily drawn away from the attitude indicator and performance instruments to enable these important tasks to be accomplished. In the process, airplane control must remain the highest priority. The attitude indicator remains the focal point of the scan.

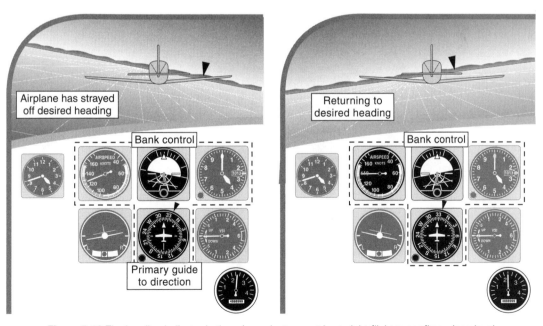

Figure 5-12 The heading indicator is the primary instrument in straight flight to confirm wings level.

Abbreviated Scans

On some occasions, it is necessary to have a fast scan, as when on final approach for landing. However, on other occasions, the scan can be more relaxed, as when cruising with the autopilot engaged.

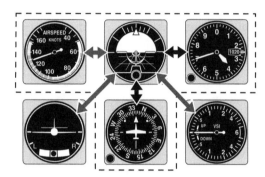

Figure 5-13
A suitable scan during
straight-and-level flight.

If you are performing other tasks while flying a constant heading, such as reading a chart, a *vertical scan* from the attitude indicator down to the heading indicator and back again is appropriate (figure 5-14).

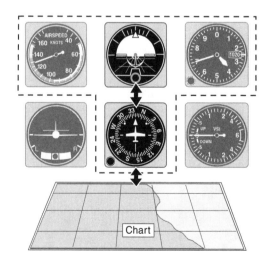

Figure 5-14
The vertical scan.

With practice, you will naturally develop suitable scans for every situation.

Attitude Instrument Flying

As mentioned, there is a direct relationship between visual and instrument attitude techniques—in fact, they are identical. In instrument flight, attitude is established with reference to the attitude indicator instead of the natural horizon—no matter what maneuver is performed.

Attitude (and Power) Control

The two parameters over which the pilot has direct *control* are attitude and power. Attitude is established on the attitude indicator. Power is set with reference to the power indicator. Configuration changes, such as flaps and landing gear selection, will also influence airplane performance.

A specific power setting and attitude will result in a predictable performance outcome, and this holds good for any airplane. For example, a PA-31 Navajo will cruise straight and level at approximately 155 knots with cruise power at 65% and a wings-level attitude with zero pitch (i.e. with the bar superimposed on the horizon). Similarly, the operations manual states that, at an average weight, a Boeing 737–300 airliner in the initial approach configuration will fly straight and level at 150 knots with a thrust setting of 69% and a pitch attitude of eight degrees. It's that simple.

Performance Is Flight Path plus Speed

As with visual attitude flight, a given flight path and speed is reflected by the performance instruments. In addition, there are standard techniques to optimize performance and accuracy when changing from one maneuver to another—for example, when leveling off at cruise altitude from a climb (attitude, power, trim, etc.).

Climb, Cruise, Descent

For most flight profiles, the power is set to a figure recommended by the manufacturer. The pilot then sets an appropriate attitude to achieve a desired flight path and speed. You will need to learn the power settings and the attitudes for your airplane. Having set the appropriate attitude, wait until the performance instruments stabilize (they lag).

Figure 5-15 Precise attitudes.

The attitude is then adjusted to achieve the primary flight path parameters:

- for the climb, the airspeed indicator is the prime reference;
- for the cruise, the altimeter is the prime reference;
- for the descent, the airspeed indicator (or sometimes the vertical speed indicator) is the prime reference; and
- for a turn, the turn coordinator is sometimes used to adjust the bank angle to achieve a certain rate, otherwise the heading indicator is used to maintain or roll out on heading.

Having set power and attitude, it is most important to fly the airplane accurately and to keep it coordinated. Table 5-1 includes a summary, in order of importance, of the primary performance instruments that are checked for each maneuver.

Maneuver	Flight Path Indicators		Comments
	Vertical	Horizontal	
Climb	ASI VSI ALT	HI TC + Ball	For climbing with constant power, (e.g. climb power), adjust attitude if required to climb at a given speed. Use 10% rate of climb as lead for leveling off (e.g. 500 fpm, start leveling off at 50 feet to go).
Straight and level	ALT VSI ASI	HI TC + Ball	Increase or decrease power and adjust attitude to regain altitude for deviations greater than 100 feet.
Descent	ASI VSI ALT	HI TC + Ball	For descending with constant power (e.g. idle power), adjust attitude if required to descend at a given airspeed. For descending at a constant IAS, adjust power to descend at a given rate. Use 10% of rate of descent at lead for leveling off (e.g. 800 fpm, start leveling off at 80 feet to go).
Climbing turn (usually no more than 15° angle of bank)	ASI VSI ALT	HI TC + Ball	Commence roll out of turn using one third of bank angle as lead (e.g. 15° angle of bank, use 5° lead to roll out on heading).
Level turn	VSI (in smooth air) ALT	HI TC + Ball	Commence rolling out of turn using one third of bank angle as lead (e.g. 30° angle of bank, use 10° lead to roll out on heading).
Descending turn	ASI VSI ALT	HI TC + Ball	Commence rolling out of turn using one third of bank angle as lead (e.g. 20° angle of bank, use 7° as lead to roll out of heading).

Table 5-1 Flight path references.

Chapter 6

Night Flight Technique

Preparation for a Possible Night Flight

Transitions

Most private pilots are likely to fly at night in the event of arriving later than expected at a destination airport at the end of a cross-country flight. Most commercial operators may well fly the total flight by night, and this is perhaps the better way to approach night flight, as you are physically and mentally prepared for night operations (provided you are properly rested). A pre-dawn departure for a daytime flight is easy if you prepare properly for the night sector (the workload gets easier as the sun rises). However, the preflight and takeoff stages for night flight are critical, and there is also the possibility of having to turn back for an emergency night landing.

Your planning should be thorough, and you should be well prepared for any eventuality. The charts should be available and visible in a reduced lighting environment. The aids should be tuned and identified. The navigation log should be up-to-date, and your position and timing should be confirmed. If you have any doubts about the suitability of a destination you had originally planned to arrive at during daylight, you must decide straightaway if you are to continue, turn back, or land immediately. Watch out for fog in valleys, especially near rivers. Generally, there is less turbulence, wind, and shear after sunset and before sunrise. Heating and thermals are minimal around dawn and dusk (this is one reason why night flight can be so pleasant).

Flying West

Flying west into the sunset is fine with respect to the clearly defined horizon, but your eyes are poorly prepared for night vision, and the lengthening shadows give a false image of terrain. If you have to turn back toward the east, there will be no horizon, no illumination, and you will have poor night vision—a bad combination. If you are equipped with bright instruments and cockpit lighting and you are a competent instrument pilot, you should have no problems.

This situation is one which should be easy to anticipate and prepare for. Even as you head west, turn up the cockpit lights and be ready in case the light level reduces when you have to turn east. Have your cockpit ready for a night sector, even if you are fairly confident of reaching your westerly destination. Avoid looking into the bright sky and setting sun, and try to prepare your eyes for night. Wear sunglasses and lower the sunshades. If you lower your seat to reduce glare, do not forget to raise it again for the approach and landing.

Flying East

Flying east in the morning can have its difficulties as the rising sun can be bright enough to obscure obstacles and high terrain. Flying east in the evening is less difficult as dusk will be shorter, darkness will fall earlier, and your night vision should be better because you will not have been looking toward the bright setting sun.

Takeoff and Landing into the Setting or Rising Sun

When taking off or landing into the setting or rising sun, try to choose a runway in a northerly or southerly direction. Make sure the windshield is clean (you did clean it before your flight, didn't you?). If you expect the sun to cause difficulties with the landing flare, delay the approach until the sun has gone down or land the other way (wind permitting). Wear quality sunglasses for the eye-shattering periods before sunset and after sunrise—sunglasses reduce glare and the time it takes to adapt to reduced contrast.

Turning

When you turn, do not look down—fly the clocks. Be careful around the end of civil twilight as there could be a clear horizon in one segment of the turn but none in the other. Cross-refer to the attitude indicator—frequently.

Preparation for a Planned Night Flight

Preflight Preparation

Night flight requires careful attention to preflight preparation and planning. While weather conditions in the vicinity of the airfield are obvious during daylight hours, the situation is different at night. Stars might be clearly visible overhead one minute, but they may be unexpectedly covered by low cloud the next, and this could have a significant effect on your departure. Study the available weather reports and forecasts, paying especial attention to any item that could affect visibility and your ability to fly at a safe operating altitude. Some of the main items to consider include:

- cloud base and amount;
- weather (e.g. rain and fog);
- temperature to dewpoint relationship (the closer they are, the more likely fog is to form as the temperature drops further); and
- wind direction and strength, including the possibility of fog being blown in and the likelihood of windshear because of the *diurnal effect* (the diurnal effect refers to a light surface wind with a strong wind at altitude resulting from reduced vertical mixing).

Check any special procedures for night operations at both the departure and arrival airfields. The en route part of the flight is similar to an IFR flight in that it requires attitude instrument flying skills. As always, the more thorough the preflight preparation, the lower the in-flight workload. Check personal equipment, including the normal daylight items (e.g. flight computer, plotter—or protractor and scale rule—and pencils). A definite requirement for night flying is a good flashlight—one for your preflight checks and another for the cockpit in case of electrical failure (ensure that the flashlight has a fresh battery).

All lines drawn on charts should preferably be in heavy black—even white light in the cockpit will probably be dimmed to ensure that good external vision is retained. If red lighting is used in the cockpit, red print on charts will be difficult to see.

Study the airport diagrams of your departure, destination, and alternate airports so you are familiar with the taxiway and runway layout. Also study the A/FD, especially the lights and services available and the hours of operation.

Radio Procedures

There is a high cockpit workload during night pattern operations, so it helps considerably if you prepare by rehearsing and memorizing all the required radio calls. Radio calls vary according to the local airfield procedures. You will need to be familiar with the differences in radio procedures and changes in responsibility for traffic separation and pattern spacing.

Airfield Availability

Many airports, both civil and military, close at night. It is always advisable to check the A/FD and NOTAMs for airport closing times—call the airport if you are unsure. Not only check your planned departure and destination airfields, but also check those airfields which might be useful as alternates en route. You must be certain that runway lighting will be available for your landing.

Weather

The weather takes on especial importance at night. All relevant information should be studied carefully, especially the airfield forecasts for your destination, as well as those for a number of alternates and your airfield of departure. Remember that the closeness of the temperature to dewpoint provides a warning of mist or fog forming as the temperature falls further during the night. There is also a risk of carburetor icing, as temperatures cool off with darkness. If flying IFR, keep in mind that strobe lights can reflect off clouds and ruin your night vision; turn off strobe lights while in cloud. If flying near lightning, turn up the cabin lights to prevent temporary blinding.

The Airplane

Check the weight and balance of the airplane and, if appropriate, the takeoff performance charts. Make sure that cargo and baggage are correctly loaded and restrained.

Preflight Inspection

Preflight inspection at night is limited by light levels on your tarmac. It is better to inspect the airplane during daylight, and it is preferable to use the same airplane you have flown that day. Alternately, pull the airplane into a lighted hanger to perform the inspection. Conduct a thorough inspection—a check of all the airplane lights is essential. In particular, check the serviceability of the instruments and lights required for night flying. It is important to visually inspect the fuel to confirm you have the quantity indicated by the gauges.

Check the cleanliness of all windows—night vision is already limited and is affected by dust and scratches on the windshield (use a chamois). Survey the area in which the airplane is parked. If the airplane is unlit, on grass, near tie-down cables or among other airplanes, you may be able to reposition it on a sealed surface with tarmac lighting and wide access. Conduct the preflight inspection using a separate flashlight. Retain the full battery charge in your personal flashlight for the flight. Not only must the airplane be checked, but the surrounding area must also be scanned for obstructions, rough or soft ground, and other airplanes. Tie-down ropes, pitot covers, control locks, and wheel chocks are more difficult to see at night.

A typical technique during the preflight check is to begin near—or in—the cockpit and to do the following:

- place the master switch on;
- check the instrument lighting and dimmers (if installed);
- check the cabin lighting;
- check the taxi light, landing lights, and anti-collision beacon (do not drain the battery unnecessarily); and
- switch on the navigation lights and leave them on for the external preflight inspection as it may be impossible to check them from inside the cockpit.

Carry out the following during the external preflight inspection:

- check all lights and their lenses for cleanliness and serviceability;
- carefully check the navigation lights (red left, green right, white tail), the taxi light, and the landing lights; and
- test any electrical stall-warning devices.

Take great care in the night preflight check—focus the flashlight on each specific item as it is checked and also run the beam of the flashlight over the airplane as a whole. If ice or frost is present, check the upper leading edge of the wing to ensure that it is also clean. Any ice, frost, or other accretion must be removed from the airplane (especially from the lift-producing surfaces and control surfaces) prior to flight. Do not forget to remove the pitot cover and to check the pitot heat.

All these simple preparations help. Allow extra time to carry out these tasks. You must not end up in a position in which you have to rush.

The Cockpit

Cockpit Lighting

The instrument lighting has priority. Set a comfortable light level and avoid reflections. (Incidentally, you will appreciate wearing a dark shirt; the traditional, white pilot's shirt is a nuisance for night flight because of the reflections on the faces of the instruments.)

Adjust the cabin lighting so that it is not distracting—low rather than high—to avoid both instrument and window reflections. Dim the cabin lights so that external vision is satisfactory and reflection from the canopy is minimized, but do not have the cabin lights so dim that you cannot see the controls or fuel selector.

Allow time for your eyes to adjust to natural night light. It may be that the apron lighting is bright and you need a bright cockpit—in this case, readjust the cockpit lighting at the run-up bay or holding point, and use the taxi time to acclimatize.

Internal Preflight

Place all items you might need in flight in a handy position, especially the flashlight, which should be placed where you can find it in complete darkness—if you need the flashlight, you will need it *right then!* Some pilots who fly regularly at night include a Velcro patch on their flashlight and headset so they can fly hands free if the occasion arises. Another option is to wear the flashlight around your neck on a long chain or cord.

Cockpit Organization

Allow extra time to settle into the cockpit and establish a comfortable lighting level. Become familiar with the location and operation of all controls and switches in this semi-darkened environment. Keep the checklist where it is readily accessible, but it is strongly recommended that you memorize all checks. Connect your headset, and adjust the intercom. Do not use a hand-held microphone for night or instrument flying unless you have no choice (i.e. emergency use).

Cockpit organization for a night cross-country flight is even more important than a day one. Have the paperwork in order—assemble it in sequence of use, fold it appropriately, have it oriented to track, and ensure that it is easy to see. Make it readily available, and stow it in sequence. If you are alone, use the copilot's seat as a working desktop, or use a knee board clipped to your leg. Have another flashlight handy for reading paperwork, or use an illuminated clipboard. Do not put the flashlight anywhere it can interfere with the magnetic field of the instruments or compass.

Front Seat Passenger

Night flying is one situation in which your flying partner can be a great aid or a great burden. Being distracted by someone sitting next to you can not only hinder you but can also seriously increase your workload and stress. A competent "copilot" is a godsend.

The Pilot

Adaptation of the Eyes to Darkness

There are some special considerations regarding your vision at night. Since your attention will be both inside and outside the cockpit during night flying, care should be taken to ensure that your eyes can function at or near maximum efficiency.

As discussed in chapter 3, it takes the eyes some minutes to adapt to darkness, and the rate at which the eyes adapt to darkness depends on the brilliance of the exposed light and the brightness and contrast of the new environment. While bright lighting within the previous few minutes has the strongest effect, bright lighting experienced for some period within the previous few hours will also have an effect.

Bright lighting is best avoided before a night flight. This can be difficult to achieve, since flight planning in a well-lit room and preflight inspection with a strong flashlight or on a well-lit tarmac will almost always be necessary. In many cases, the best that can be achieved is to dim the cockpit lighting prior to taxiing and to avoid looking at bright lights during the few minutes prior to takeoff.

Avoid looking at strobes or landing lights. In particular, strobes can be a major distraction in mist, cloud, or rain.

Night vision can be affected by a lack of oxygen, so ensure that you use oxygen when flying above 10,000 feet MSL, and preferably above 5,000 feet at night. Avoid smoking before flight as the carbon monoxide will displace some of the oxygen in your blood, thereby reducing your night vision.

There are some occasions when bright cockpit lighting can actually help preserve your vision. This can be the case during an instrument flight when flying in the vicinity of electrical storms. Nearby lightning flashes can temporarily degrade your adaptation to darkness and your vision, particularly if the flashes are in contrast to a dim cockpit. Bright lighting in the cockpit can minimize the effect of bright lightning flashes, and although your external vision will not be as good as it would be with dim cockpit lighting, you will avoid being temporarily blinded by lightning flashes.

Electrical storms should be avoided by at least 10 NM. If thunderstorms are forecast in your area, stay on the ground.

Self-Compensation

Your paperwork needs to be well organized, and you need to allow for the fact that instruments and charts will be illuminated by artificial light.

The airfields from which you normally operate will look different at night. The airfields with which you are unfamiliar will be even more so at night. You will need to ensure that you are at the right place, and you will need to pre-brief yourself on the taxiways, runways, and lighting.

The Airfield

Always have a plan for night flight—even for a local flight. In your plan, include runway in use, taxi routes, run-up bay, holding points, radio frequencies, radio calls, and the flight profile. Restudy the layout of the airfield, the runways for night operations, any night pattern restrictions (directions and attitudes), NOTAMs, and possible wind and weather implications. Check the location of the illuminated windsock, and check the operation and layout of the airfield lighting. Select lit features to assist with pattern orientation and spacing.

Engine Start

Make sure you have the parking brake on before starting the engine, especially as movement of an airplane is less noticeable at night. The rotating beacon or navigation lights should be turned on just prior engine start to warn any person nearby that the engine(s) are about to start. Some schools flash the taxi or landing lights—check the *standard operating procedures* (SOPs) for your flying school.

Keep a good lookout before starting the engine—a spinning propeller is more difficult to see at night. Passengers have been struck while taking a short-cut to the cabin or while transferring from one airplane to another. Do not start the engine—not even the engine on the side opposite the door—before all passengers are on board.

After start, check outside to make sure that the airplane is not moving, and then complete your after-start checks.

Taxiing

The responsibility for collision avoidance always rests with the pilot. Use the taxi light, and only switch it off if it is about to point at other airplanes. The taxi light not only helps you see obstructions, but it also makes your airplane more visible. It is usual to turn on the taxi light before moving from the parking area; this serves to warn other crews that you are about to taxi forward.

Taxi slowly and carefully. Look at the wing tip to check your speed—imagine someone is walking alongside your airplane and match their walking pace.

Taxiing at night requires additional attention for the following reasons:

- distances are more difficult to judge at night—stationary lights may appear closer than they really are;
- speed is very deceptive at night—there is a tendency to taxi too fast; and
- other airplanes and obstacles are less visible at night—an airplane ahead on the taxiway may be showing just a single white tail light and that light may be lost among other lights.

Taxiway lighting will be either two lines of blue edge lights, or one line of green centerline lights. At most major airports, these lights have variable intensity settings and may be adjusted at the pilot's request or when deemed necessary by the controller. Taxi guide lines may be marked on hard surfaces.

Stay in the center of the taxiway to preserve wing-tip clearance, but you may like to taxi slightly off-center to avoid bouncing the nosewheel over the centerline lights. The ground reflection of the wing-tip navigation lights, especially on high-wing airplanes, is useful in judging the clearance between the wing tips and obstacles at the side of the taxiway. Look at the wing tip where taxiway lights and reflected lighting will help you to judge your speed.

If you are at all unfamiliar with the airport, request a progressive taxi (ask for taxi instructions) from ATC. This is especially helpful at night, as the sea of lights can be confusing to even the most experienced pilot.

If there is *any* doubt about your taxi path, slow down or stop. If you stop, apply the parking brake. The traditional law of aviation states there is *no* excuse for a taxiing accident. The landing lights may be used to provide a better view ahead, but they draw more power and may overheat without cooling airflow. Some taxiways run parallel to the runway, so avoid shining your bright lights into the eyes of a pilot who is taking off, landing, or taxiing. Avoid looking into the landing lights of other airplanes yourself—doing so will seriously degrade your night vision for a few minutes.

Complete a normal instrument check while taxiing:

- turning left, skidding right, wings level, HI decreasing, ADF needle tracking; and
- turning right, skidding left, wings level, HI increasing, ADF needle tracking.

Run-Up

Ensure that the parking brakes are on—an airplane can easily move during the power check, and at night there are few visual cues to alert the pilot. Complete the normal run-up checks and pretakeoff vital actions. Adjust the lighting now that you are away from the tarmac. During the pretakeoff checks, do not have the cabin lighting so bright that it impairs your night vision. The flashlight can be used if bright cabin lighting is not desired.

Pay special attention to the fuel selection, as the fuel selector may be in a dim part of the cockpit. Ensure that any item required in flight is in a handy position. While the airplane is stationary, check that the heading indictor is aligned with the compass. Although included in the normal daylight pretakeoff checks, this check is especially important at night as the heading indictor will be a primary reference for direction—both in the pattern area and en route.

Preset as many communication frequencies as possible to reduce your workload after liftoff. Use whatever NAVAIDs you have, tuning and identifying each one.

Holding Point

Taxi to the holding point, which may have special lights or markings. If you have a combined taxi and landing light, avoid pointing it toward landing airplanes. Check the windsock, and anticipate the effect of wind on your takeoff and pattern. Take some time here (the "ten-second think") to consider the effect of different wind directions and speeds throughout the pattern and the allowances you will need to make. Wind at pattern altitude will be stronger than on the surface. Turn on the strobes and transponder. Turn on the pitot heat, and leave it on for all night flying operations. After you have received a takeoff clearance, line up, turn on the landing light, and turn off the taxi light. Do not intrude on the runway until you are ready, you have a clearance (if appropriate), and the runway and its approaches are clear of conflicting airplanes.

A final check of cabin lighting should be made. Ensure that it is adjusted to a suitable level and that it is bright enough to see the major items and instruments in the cockpit, but not so bright as to seriously affect your outside vision.

Night Takeoff

When ready to line up for takeoff, make any necessary radio calls, turn on the landing light, and look carefully for other traffic on the ground and in the air. Clear the approach path to the runway, checking both left and right—*Clear left, clear right.*

Conditions are often calm at night, making either direction on the runway suitable for operations. Ensure that the approach areas at both ends of the runway are clear. Self-brief your emergency actions.

Check the windsock. Do not be in a hurry to roll. If necessary, ask for thirty seconds on the threshold when you call *ready*, so that the controller knows you need the time to prepare for takeoff.

Figure 6-1
Night takeoff.

Do not waste runway length when lining up. Line up on the centerline with the nose-wheel straight. Check that the HI agrees with the runway direction and that the AI is erect. With your feet well away from the brakes and on the rudder pedals, smoothly apply full power.

During a night takeoff, directional control is best achieved with reference to the center of the far end of the runway. Keep the runway light pattern symmetrical. Runway centerline markings may also assist. Quickly check rpm and MAP and that the ASI is reading. Avoid over-controlling during the ground run. Relax.

The takeoff is the same at night as it is by day. At liftoff speed, rotate positively to the initial climb attitude. Fly the airplane away from the ground, accelerate to climb speed, and adopt the normal climb attitude. Watch out for reflections from the landing light and strobes if there is mist or drizzle. The big difference between day and night takeoff operations is that, at night, visual reference to the ground is quickly lost after liftoff, and any tendency to settle back onto the ground will not be as easily noticed.

As soon as the airplane is airborne and positively climbing, retract the landing gear, and transfer your attention to the attitude indicator. Transfer to instruments before losing the last visual references, which will typically be the last set of runway lights—but do not lower the nose. The first 300 to 400 feet of the climb-out should be totally on instruments, and you should remain on instruments until you are high enough to regain usable visual references. Retract the flaps above 200 feet AGL, and turn off the landing lights.

Maintain the normal takeoff pitch attitude, and keep the wings level on the attitude indicator. The ASI should be checked to ensure that a suitable airspeed is being maintained on the climb-out, with minor adjustments made on the AI as necessary. When well away from the ground and comfortable in the climb-out, the HI can be checked for heading. You may now adjust the power and turn off the boost pump.

Normally, a straight climb path is maintained until 500 feet AGL before turning to the crosswind leg (unless there is a good reason to turn earlier, such as high ground). Depending on your departure track and the 25 NM minimum sector altitude (MSA), you may elect to climb to 1,000 or 1,500 feet before making a turn. The direction of turn must conform to the pattern for night operations. You cannot turn opposite to the pattern until beyond 3 NM or above 1,500 feet.

With little or no natural horizon, the instruments become very important. If glare from the landing lights or strobes is distracting, turn them off when established in the climb. Mist, haze, smoke, or cloud will cause distracting reflections. Some common errors are as follows:
- letting the airplane bank slightly so it is no longer aligned with the runway during the after-takeoff checks;
- lowering the nose while maintaining visual contact with the runway; and
- relaxing back pressure on the control column as the power is reduced, thereby allowing the attitude to decrease and the airplane to settle into a reduced climb or even a shallow descent.

Departure

When the airplane is stabilized on its climb path, position the airplane over a known location, and record the time. If the airplane is still climbing, the ground speed and elapsed-time calculations will be in error. Either plan for the climb (time and average ground speed) or depart from overhead the airfield or from a fix at cruise altitude and airspeed.

En Route

The en route phase of the flight should be very similar to an IFR flight. Remain inside the 25 NM MSA as you climb until you are above the lowest safe altitude for the first leg, then depart on track and continue your climb to your cruising level. Departure procedures and maneuvering to intercept track can be demanding. Use your autopilot to free your hands so you can complete your checks, log your departure time, and make the necessary radio calls. Monitor what the autopilot is doing, and in particular, keep attitude in your scan.

When settled in the cruise, tune the primary tracking NAVAID to the next station, and keep a secondary aid tuned to the nearest suitable airfield.

Tidy up the cockpit for the next sector, but do not allow yourself to relax too much as you need to stay aware of weather and your position in relation to other airplanes. Review the activity required at the next turning or reporting point and, when ready, have a basic descent plan in mind for your destination.

Navigation Technique

There was once an advertisement with two chocolates travelling on a train; the first chocolate had a map, and the second one asked where they were. The first replied that he didn't know—the train was not marked on the map! We are in exactly the same boat (or airplane in our case). You can only map read if you know where you are. More correctly, you can only accurately fix your position if you know your approximate position.

How do we know our approximate position? (Yes, GPS gives precise positions without an intermediate step, but what if the coordinates are incorrect, the battery fails, or the signal is lost?) We know our approximate position by starting from a known position at a known time. By noting speed, direction, and time, and allowing for forecast winds, we know where we should be at a certain elapsed time. We then look at a map for features and try to match these with the same pattern on the ground. Pattern matching is one of the pilot's greatest learned skills. If we read from ground to map, there is no way to pattern match as everything on the map will have the same relative importance.

The navigation cycle involves marking significant features on the map, both on track and cross track. Note the expected time of arrival and then memorize the pattern that the features should make. The mental overlay will match a pattern on the ground within normal navigation tolerances. The pattern will come into focus, and minor updates on progress can then be made—we leapfrog from one feature to the next.

At night, visual navigation is made difficult as a pattern of lights can be entirely different to a pattern of features on a map. Therefore, accuracy of flying and accurate log keeping are essential—timing is vital.

Trusted features include:

- coastlines with inlets and peninsulas;
- major rivers and lakes (but be aware of possible changes with heavy rains and dry seasons);
- major highways;
- the relationship between country towns (by this is meant the pattern made by the relative position of each town rather than the shape made by each cluster of lights);
- lit obstructions in remote areas (e.g. transmission towers);
- airfield beacons and PAL (yes, use it to confirm position when overflying, and plan your route via airfields with PAL if you can); and
- nautical beacons and lighthouses (they are shown on aeronautical charts).

Add any information gained from NAVAIDs to the visual navigation picture, but still maintain the visual scan and log.

Assembling the Complete Picture

The pilot's primary role is to make decisions. The quality of the decision depends on the quality of the information—the most recent, most relevant, most complete, and most accurate. Given this data, the quality of a decision depends on the training, experience, and self-discipline of the pilot who is processing the data. At night, the pilot's task is a little more difficult because of the paucity of visual information. However, if the pilot assembles all available information, the task is little different from daytime flight. In the meanwhile, accurate control of the airplane attitude and heading remains fundamental.

Fly the airplane and assemble navigation information. Look for features from map to outside. Interpret the aids, and use them to confirm the visual data. Make sure you are at or above the lowest safe altitude and on track before leaving overhead the departure airfield.

Heading, Time, and Airspeed

Ever since the mailplanes first explored the possibility of reliable night and instrument flight, a basic law was realized—fly accurate heading and airspeed and monitor the progress of time. Every other aid is used to confirm or adjust this relationship. It is the fundamental principle of pilot navigation. To fly an accurate heading, keep the wings level, and quickly correct deviations. To fly airspeed, set the optimum power and altitude, and confirm the true airspeed (TAS). Monitor the passing of ground features to check ground speed and track and to amend ETAs (also use aids to refine this).

The navigation cycle at night is no different from during the day, except there is reduced visual information (this can be a good thing), and you cannot afford to waste time on reading. However, in many parts of the country, there is often zero visual information for a while. Here, the options are assembling whatever NAVAID information is available, flying an accurate heading and speed, and noting the progress of time.

It is vital to keep a flight log of fixes and times so that you have an updated basis for diversion, rerouting, or returning to your destination. Use the aids and assemble all of the information. Believe the majority of aids, if they are similar. GPS can be accurate to within feet but also inaccurate by tens of miles. Keep it honest by making mental approximations and then believe what it says. Do not look for unnecessary work. Fix your position every ten minutes or so, and fly accurately and enjoy the scenery in between position fixes.

As we continue along track, the process is one of seeing those visual features that can be positively identified. There is a danger of using unexpected information because when we read the map, we do not know what is going to be visible or what features will look like.

Visual navigation at night is highly unreliable. Use all visual and NAVAID data, in support of heading, time, and airspeed. If there is a disagreement, believe the majority but only if the majority agrees with your mental progress.

Descent

To make a visual approach at night, you must not descend below the lowest safe altitude/minimum sector altitude (MSA) (or minimum vector altitude (MVA) in a radar environment) for that route segment until the airplane is established as follows:
- clear of cloud;
- in sight of ground or water;
- with a flight visibility of not less than 3 miles; and
- either within the airfield circling area (3 NM of the airport reference point (ARP)) or within 5 NM of an airfield and established on centerline and not below the VASIS approach slope (7 NM for a runway with ILS).

Even if the approach controller clears you to make a visual approach or to maintain terrain clearance visually, do not deviate from the inbound track until within 3 NM of the threshold.

Activate the PAL.

Night Arrival

When approaching the airport to enter the traffic pattern and land, it is important to identify the runway lights and other airport lighting as early as possible. If you are unfamiliar with the airport layout, sighting of the runway may be difficult until very close-in, due to the maze of lights observed in the area. Fly toward the rotating beacon until the lights outlining the runway are distinguishable. To fly a traffic pattern of proper size and direction, the runway threshold and runway-edge lights must be positively identified. Once the airport lights are seen, these lights should be kept in sight throughout the approach.

Distance may be deceptive at night, due to limited lighting conditions. This also applies to the estimation of altitude and speed. Consequently, more dependence must be placed on flight instruments, particularly the altimeter and the airspeed indicator.

Every effort should be made to maintain the recommended airspeeds and execute the approach and landing in the same manner as during the day. A low, shallow approach is definitely inappropriate during a night operation. The altimeter and VSI should be constantly cross-checked against the airplane's position along the base leg and final approach.

There is a tendency to overbank at night. Keep your head movements to a minimum, especially while rolling into or out of a turn. Move your head slowly. When the runway and airfield lights are seen, they should be referred to frequently. Well-lit landmarks may also be useful for positioning in the pattern.

Allow for drift on the crosswind leg, and level off using normal instrument procedures. Accurately maintain altitude, and carefully scan outside before making any turns. A good lookout for other airplanes must be maintained at all times, and the usual radio procedures must be followed.

Recognize and respond to the navigation lights of other airplanes (refer to figure 6-2). Green to red is not safe, and this will be the situation if two airplanes are flying parallel on downwind. An especially careful lookout will need to be maintained. Listening to radio transmissions will help you maintain a mental picture of what else is happening in the pattern.

Complete the prelanding checks and assess the wind.

I would recommend turning on the landing light on downwind—provided it won't shine into the eyes of a pilot on final. If the light is activated on downwind, you have time to check that it is working. If it isn't, you can mentally prepare for a no-light landing. If it works okay, you can adjust to any reflections and distractions before you settle on base and final.

If you leave the landing light off until the final checks, it can cause a momentary change in the appearance of the runway and threshold, and this will affect your judgment for a few seconds at a crucial time. Better to have the configuration set early, including propeller, gear and flaps—except the last stage for landing.

As you should (and probably do) during day flights, nominate a precise threshold speed for your approach. Say to yourself, "I will fly this final approach in the landing configuration, stabilized and trimmed, to cross the threshold at … knots."

The turn from downwind to base leg should be made at the normal position with reference to the runway lights and any approach lighting. The descent on base leg should be planned so that the turn to final commences at about 600 to 700 feet AGL, ideally with a 20° bank angle—certainly no more than 30°.

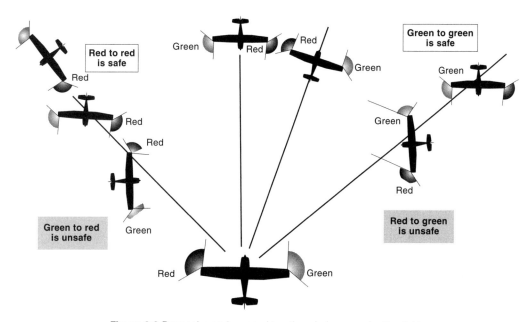

Figure 6-2 Recognize and respond to other airplanes navigation lights.

Night Approach

At night, ask yourself, "*Is the threshold the same distance below the horizon as it would be during a daytime approach?*" This is the only true measure of the correct approach path.

Note. This is sometimes referred to as the *x-height*.

The aspect of the runway will change, the threshold will get wider, and so the ratio of width to height will also change. If you try to keep a constant aspect ratio, you will be overshooting. Complete the final checks, and make a positive decision to continue or go-around.

Decision

Proceed on base—provided it feels comfortable and you are not at all uneasy. On final, line up on the centerline and ask yourself if everything is "in the groove." If there is any doubt, go-around and set up another pattern. If the approach is looking good, make a conscious decision to commit to landing. Lower landing flaps, reduce to the planned threshold speed and re-trim. Now finesse the approach for accuracy of speed and flight path to the aim point.

When the decision is made to commit to the approach, the airplane is configured with landing flaps, propellers full fine, *landing light on*, and landing gear three greens confirmed. The airplane is trimmed and will maintain a stabilized approach. Speed should be V_{REF} (aim for a tolerance of +5 knots minus *nothing*).

Now your references and techniques change. Your scan is primarily focused on the runway for height, centerline, and attitude. Scan "*aimpoint, attitude, airspeed.*"

Any tendency to drift off the extended centerline can be counteracted with coordinated turns. Drift can be laid off if a crosswind exists—use rudder to assist. Be prepared for wind changes as the descent progresses. The difference between the wind at 1,000 feet AGL and at ground level is likely to be more pronounced at night than by day. It is common for the wind speed to decrease and the wind direction to back as the airplane descends.

The aim point should stay in the same position in the windshield. Correct this with attitude. Maintain airspeed during the final approach by adjusting power. Remember—the runway aspect will change as you get closer. It does not stay constant, even on a constant approach path. The only constant is the distance of the threshold (aim point) below the horizon.

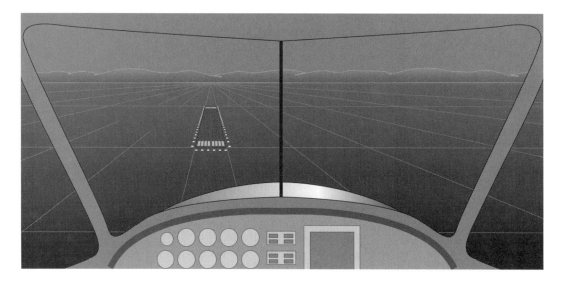

Figure 6-3 Final approach—dusk.

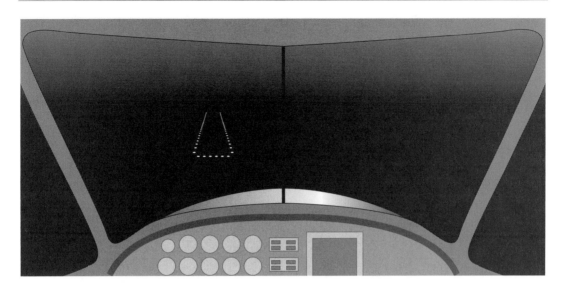

Figure 6-4 Runway aspect—three-degree glide slope.

You may not have a visual horizon at night, but you can still picture the distance of the threshold below the horizon by imagining the point at which the runway lights converge. This is the horizon.

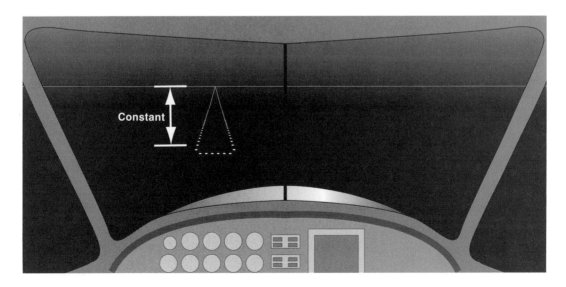

Figure 6-5 The runway edges converge at the horizon.

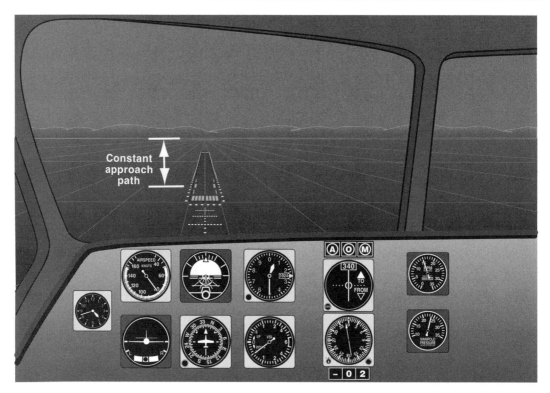

Figure 6-6 A well executed final approach path.

Judgment is subtle, but you will find that, with practice, you will instinctively feel that you are high or low or are getting either way. It is vital to reinforce this judgment by flying fairly frequently so that it becomes a repeatable performance.

When you feel that the approach is correct, you can refine the approach by selecting a specific aim point—a point 200 feet in from the threshold corresponding to the central space between the first pair of white side lights is recommended. The aim point is the point at which your eyes would impact the runway if you did not flare. Continue the final approach, making continuous small adjustments. Do not forget that the airplane is equipped with a rudder which is most effective in assisting lateral corrections on final. Use it in a coordinated way with aileron inputs to point the nose. As you approach the threshold, the runway lights near the threshold should start moving down the windshield. Certain runway features may become visible in the cone of the landing light.

During poor visibility conditions and particularly during night approaches, make doubly sure you do not underrun your glide path (do this by periodically checking the altimeter and the vertical speed indicator). Set your own VFR minimums relative to the airport elevation, making sure you do not hit the 50 ft mark until you are over the runway threshold.

Also, using a descent rate not in excess of 400 to 500 fpm helps to prevent an inadvertently steep flight path. Even on clear but moonless nights, an approach into a black hole airport out in the boondocks can be extremely hazardous, unless the flight instruments are scanned systematically until reaching the runway—because of the visual illusions involved.

Flare, Hold-Off, and Landing at Night

The best guide to flare height and round-out is the runway perspective given by the runway edge lighting. As the airplane descends toward the runway, the runway edge lighting you see in your peripheral vision will appear to rise.

The appearance of the ground can sometimes be deceptive at night, so even when using landing lights, use the runway lighting as your main guide in the flare and hold-off, both for depth perception and for tracking guidance. (For this reason, your introductory landings may be made without the use of landing lights.)

Continue to the threshold. At this point, do not look at the runway illuminated by the landing light, but transfer your gaze to the *center of the far end of the runway*. Gently raise the nose of the airplane until the flight path changes toward this point. Straighten the airplane with rudder using aileron to prevent any bank, and reduce the power. As you reduce the power, maintain back pressure on the control column as if you were trying to actually reach the far end of the runway. Lower the upwind wing to prevent any drift. The airplane will land itself.

Do not freeze or tense up—you have a job to do. Wiggle your fingers and not only look at the aim point but also scan back and forth to the far end of the runway. Do not become focused on one point. There is a common tendency to flare and hold off a little too high in the first few night landings, but this tendency is soon corrected. The runway perspective on touchdown should resemble that on liftoff, and an appreciation of this is best achieved by looking well ahead toward the far end of the runway. Avoid trying to see the runway under the nose of the airplane—this will almost certainly induce a tendency to fly into the ground before rounding out.

As the airplane is flared for landing, the power should be gradually reduced as the airplane enters the hold-off phase—but not before flaring. Check the throttle is fully closed as the airplane settles onto the ground. Keep straight during the landing ground run with rudder, and keep the wings level with aileron.

Maintain the centerline until the airplane has slowed to taxi speed. Brake if necessary, and look at the wing tip to confirm a slow speed. Taxi clear of the runway, stop the airplane, set the brakes to park, and complete the after-landing checks.

During landings without the use of landing lights, the round-out may be started when the runway lights at the far end of the runway first appear to be rising higher than the nose of the airplane. This demands a smooth and very timely round-out; it also requires you to feel for the runway surface, using power and pitch changes as necessary, for the airplane to settle slowly to the runway. Blackout landings should always be included in night pilot training as an emergency procedure.

Night landings have a special element of risk. Part of the reason for this is that pilots often neglect to maintain their night flying proficiency. But don't kid yourself—night flying can be as tough as flying on instruments:

- Periodically undertake some dual night flying with an instructor, and prepare for the unexpected. Shoot some landings without panel lights and, where permitted, without landing lights.
- At night, traffic patterns must be flown with extra care. Allow plenty of time to do your prelanding checklist before entering the pattern.
- In the pattern, maintain the recommended speeds—do not exceed them. Give yourself plenty of time to prepare for the approach and landing.
- A long, low final is to be avoided at all costs and especially at night. The presence of unseen obstacles around the airport is a prime reason to always check flight information publications for airport details before you launch. Know where those obstacles are before, not after.
- On approach, make sure your glide path is high enough to stay well clear of all obstacles—not just the ones you can see.
- Be sure your heading indicator is aligned with the magnetic compass. It will help you locate the runway you'll want to use.
- Set the heading bug; it will help you fly a square pattern at night.
- Set your altimeter. Remember, a one-inch decrease in barometric pressure means your altimeter reading is about one-thousand feet higher than your actual altitude.
- On final, take advantage of VASI guidance where available. Never allow a "low" indication to appear at night. Get back up to your glide path immediately, or take it around and try again.
- With ATC permission, you can also make use of an ILS to guide you to your landing runway at night.
- If runway lights become fuzzy on final, beware. You may be seeing the effects of ground fog which can lead to "suddenly" reduced visibility as you near the runway for touchdown. Fog can form in minutes, obscuring all or part of any runway. An alternate airport may be your best bet.
- "Atmospherics" can change colors, light intensities, and even depth perception. Even when "atmospherics" are not a problem, optical illusions can be.
- A lighted area may be mistaken for a runway; one airport may be mistaken for another, resulting in landing at the wrong facility. Landings on roads and parking lots are not unheard of when lighting patterns create confusion.
- To cut costs, some airport lighting is now radio controlled. Be sure you know how to use them; know the specific instructions for the runway lighting installed where

you're landing. Flight information publications have the data, including frequencies and procedures to activate these lighting systems as well as how to raise or lower the light intensity. Many systems turn themselves off after 15 minutes. Don't be caught on short final when the lights go out. If you are caught, go around, turn the lights back on, and try again.

- Never attempt a landing at an unlighted airport, no matter how well you think you know it. If in doubt about lighting at your destination, do not be embarrassed. Call Flight Service.
- At a tower-controlled airport, you may also have the option of asking for the raising or lowering of runway light intensity, if needed.
- You can also ask them to "kill the rabbit," that is, extinguish the sequential strobe approach lights if they become distracting, which they often do when you're close to the runway.
- An easy way to enhance your ability to see outside obstacles is to dim interior cockpit lighting. Know the color coding: "aviation red" lighting or white strobes mean obstacles to air navigation.
- Carry a couple of flashlights. They're awfully easy to lose down under a seat somewhere, especially when you need one. Keep one around your neck on a lanyard.
- Flashlights should be in working order. Experienced pilots carry spare bulbs and batteries.
- Also important at night is a spare pair of glasses. Your eyes work harder at night and it's going to be tough if you lose a contact lens or break your only pair of glasses in flight.
- At an airport that's not very busy, it's often best to "drag the field" at fifty to one-hundred feet on the first pass to check for obstructions and animals at night. Runways hold the day's heat and animals love to congregate there as the cool night progresses. Also, runways are favorite places for clandestine drag racing.

Touch-and-Go Landing

For a touch-and-go landing, you can reselect the flaps after touchdown to the takeoff setting (up) and reapply power. Be careful when retracting the flaps, as it is possible in some airplanes to inadvertently select the landing gear—especially at night. You may need to retrim.

Be careful not to look inside the cockpit for too long. Try to feel and reach the controls and only look as a quick check. It is useful to practice and remember how long for electric trim or how much wheel movement it takes to approximately reset the trim from landing to takeoff.

Reintroduce full power, and keep straight as you do so. Keep heading for the black hole at the other end of the runway. Continue for a normal takeoff, rotate on speed, focus on the attitude indicator, watch the heading indicator, and be ready for an engine failure.

Keep in mind that the FAA night currency requirements mandate landings be made to a full stop.

Go-Around at Night

The flying technique for a go-around at night is the same as by day, except that it is done primarily by reference to instruments. The runway lighting available during the latter stages of the approach are no longer visible when full power is applied and pitch attitude is raised. There may be strong pitch and yaw tendencies because of the power increase, and these must be controlled (with reference to the flight instruments). Retract the landing gear. Hold the desired attitude on the AI, monitor vertical performance on the altimeter, monitor airspeed, and maintain centerline. Partially retract the flaps with a positive rate of climb.

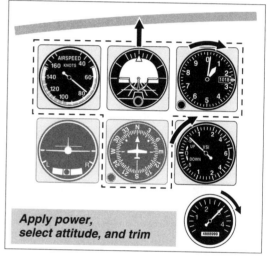

Figure 6-7 Night go-around—power and attitude.

Night Patterns

Continue the initial climb to 500 feet AGL, look for airplanes that may be joining crosswind, and commence a normal climbing turn *on instruments*. Leave the boost (fuel) pump on for all night patterns unless advised otherwise by the flight manual.

When established on crosswind, slowly look back at the runway to orient yourself and to see the general picture. To look back any earlier is risky because you have to turn further to see the runway. It is more difficult to maintain a constant attitude as you do this, and you also risk the *leans*. Do not move your head quickly, especially if you are rolling into or out of a turn—the combined motion can induce powerful illusions.

To turn downwind, return to instruments with some allowance for wind. Use the heading needle as a guide. Remember that the airplane is *flown* with reference to the instruments and *positioned* with respect to the runway. The airplane is only *flown* visually on final approach and during the initial takeoff run.

The turn to downwind is initiated with allowance for turn radius. The bank angle is adjusted to roll out at normal lateral spacing from the runway (with the wing tip overlapping or tracking down the runway). There is a need to scan the instruments for attitude and performance. Watch the runway to assess spacing, adjust heading accordingly, and look for other pattern traffic. There is a tendency to think you are closer than you should be and to over correct.

Complete the downwind or prelanding checks—you will appreciate the value of not having to read a checklist. Hold the gear lever until you have three greens.

Be aware of the visual illusion that can happen on downwind with regard to height and spacing (refer to figure 6-8).

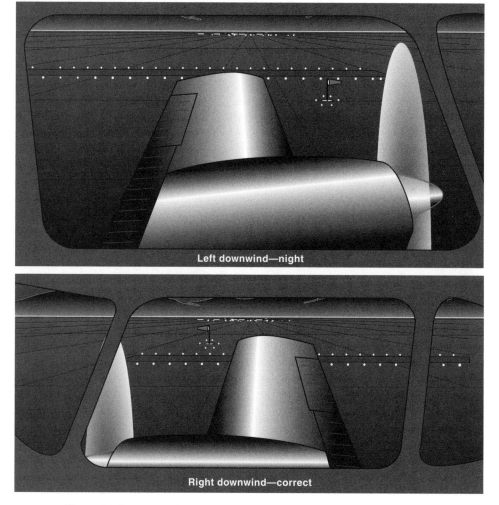

Figure 6-8 Perception of altitude can be skewed between right and left patterns.

As an added guide for turning base, I start the stopwatch abeam the threshold and turn base at 30–40 seconds (when the airplane is on a line 45° from the runway threshold). Initiate the base turn as you would during the day, but fly with reference to the attitude indicator. Simply adjust the power, set the attitude in bank and pitch, lower the flaps if appropriate, adjust the attitude, and trim the airplane. There is a need to scan from the attitude indicator to the performance instruments to the runway and then back again—similar to the downwind turn. This is a selective radial scan (as you were taught in instrument flying), but it is widened to encompass the runway. Be careful not to let the nose drop as the power is reduced.

When the attitude, power, and configuration are set for the approach, accurately trim the airplane. Adjust the power to correct for any feeling or tendency of being too high or too low and for any expected headwind on final approach. Make an associated adjustment to the attitude to maintain airspeed. Turn final early, and look out for other traffic when on final or on the runway.

Chapter 7

Abnormal Operations at Night

Risk Management

First ventures into a dark night can be traumatic, especially for passengers—but these first ventures need not be so. Night flying is not inherently difficult; nor is it more dangerous. It is the same as flight by day, but it requires more active scans of the attitude indicator and the performance instruments. Night flight and situational awareness do require concentration and cockpit organization so that your mind is not diverted from important tasks. Night flying is unforgiving of error and inattention. Furthermore, your senses can become confused. The essence of safe and pleasant night flight is preparation.

Workload

The more workload there is in flight, the less safe you are. You need to think carefully about workload when choosing an airplane for night flying—it is preferable to fly a well-equipped airplane with autopilot, redundant systems, and NAVAIDs. It is usual to have a turn coordinator or turn indicator as the backup for attitude indicator failure or vacuum failure. If an airplane with a standby attitude indicator is available, use it—it's life assurance, as flying on partial panel significantly increases the workload and the risk of loss of control. A heading indicator is a second-class alternative to a magnetically aligned heading indicator. Fixed card RBIs also cause added workload as they are much more difficult to interpret. If you have a choice, fly an airplane with an RMI or HSI. At night and in IMC, they can be a necessity, not a luxury.

Use the flight aids as they are designed to be used, and use the spare capacity they give you to manage the flight—I would not fly solo IMC or night cross-country without a serviceable autopilot. Do not trust GPS as the sole source of navigation data.

Briefing and Using the Front Seat Passenger

Like the GPS and other devices, the front seat passenger can be a godsend or a nuisance and will either ease or add to the cockpit workload significantly (and the workload for single-pilot night flight is already high). If sensible use is made of this side-by-side aid, your flights can be a pleasure. If your front seat passenger is involved in the planning stage of a flight and is briefed of his or her duties, you will have a team player who can help make night flying much easier. Tell your front seat passenger to act as your watchdog and to let you know if you miss a radio call, misinterpret an instruction, mis-set a heading or forget an assigned altitude.

Conversely, if you are the front seat passenger (spouse especially), you can make or break a night flight and the pilot—you can make the pilot smile or scream. There is a delicate balance between constructive and critical commentary. Do not add to a pilot's workload by diverting attention toward menial things. Do not add to a pilot's stress levels by complaining of lateness or by trying to hurry him or her. Do keep children under control and, above all, do not question a pilot's decision to turn back or to land before dark.

Selection of Route and Cruising Level

As well as fuel, terrain, and navigation considerations, select the route that gives best visual references and escape options in the event of loss of power, lighting failure, or loss of NAVAIDs and communications. Flying coastal routes offers the best options, as the terrain is off to one side making visual navigation easier. Avoid long sectors over mountainous terrain. Stay near highways or rivers in remote areas.

Things that May Go Wrong in the Flight

Inadvertent/Unplanned Night Flight

If you run out of daylight while cruising, immediately climb above the lowest safe altitude. Fly on instruments if the horizon disappears. Engage the autopilot. Turn on the cockpit lights. Tune and identify the aids. Continue your planned track if the destination has lighting and an NDB; otherwise, divert to the nearest suitable alternate. Check the fuel situation. Tell ATC what you are doing.

Inadvertently Entering Cloud

If you inadvertently enter cloud, select the following:
- pitot heat on;
- carburetor heat on; and
- strobe lights off.

Check that all seat belts (yours and those of your passengers) are fastened. Stabilize the flight path (constant attitude and power), trim carefully, and engage the autopilot. If you have no rudder trim, keep the airplane coordinated with rudder (an airplane that is uncoordinated—sideslipping—will confuse both your inner ear and the autopilot). If there is lightning or dark clouds, turn on—or turn up—the cockpit flood lights. Stop looking out, and keep your head still. Start a regular scan of the instruments so that you are already on the clocks for a period before losing sight of the horizon.

Make a note of which direction you would turn if you had to descend (i.e. the direction which offers the lowest safe altitude and is clear of hills). Note the actual cloud base when entering.

Temporary Uncertainty of Position

Do not trust GPS as the sole source of data. At night, it is easier to lose the plot—to lose awareness of where you are or, conversely, to over-anticipate and panic about a lack of visual information. Be patient. If you have planned well and logged the last fix, you can fly an accurate heading and anticipate what is due next. You will be right. In the meantime, use other aids to check your progress. If an expected feature does not appear on time (and at night it may not appear at all), plan ahead for the next one. *Heading, time, and airspeed* are the navigation tenets of the old pilots—and these tenets still hold true. Do not forget the cockpit house-keeping duties. Maintain regular systems scans, and in particular do a regular "CLEAROF" check. (Do not forget to check and realign the HI):

Compass	Align the direction indicator.
Log	Log departure time from known position on map(s) and flight plan. Maintain a progressive flight log.
Engine	Engine temperature and pressure—check in the green. Check correct power setting for cruise. Lean mixture.
Altitude	Check local altimeter setting and safely clear of terrain. Check cruising level.
Radio	Check on correct frequency. Radio calls made if appropriate. NAVAIDs tuned, identified, and tested.
Orientation	General direction correct and map aligned with flight path.
Fuel	Selected on correct tank (times logged). In balance. Amended arrival fuel state.

Figure 7-1 *"CLEAROF"* check.

Maintain a flight log with confirmed positions and time. Whatever you are doing and whenever you do it, *keep the wings level*—a very slight wing down is the most common cause of a wandering heading, inaccurate navigation, a potentially diverging flight path, and, ultimately, a spiral dive. The best means of reducing workload and keeping the wings level is the autopilot. Center the heading bug and engage the autopilot.

If the GPS fails or if the next feature does not appear as expected, double-check the heading you have been flying, the time and the position you should have achieved, and the probable direction of error. If there is a NAVAID nearby, track to pass overhead, and plan your journey from there. Inform air traffic control of your predicament and intentions. If you cannot track to overhead, tune two NAVAIDs to gain an approximate fix. Note the time, check the HI is aligned, and turn toward your next waypoint. *If in doubt, call for assistance.*

Emergency Radio Procedures

Request assistance whenever you have any serious doubts regarding the safety of a flight. Transmission should be slow and distinct, with each word pronounced clearly so that there is no need for repetition. This of course should apply to all radio transmissions, but it is especially important in emergency situations.

Declaring an Emergency

As pilot in command, it is your responsibility to ensure the safety of your passengers, yourself, and your airplane. As pilot in command, you have a duty of care to your passengers whether they are fare paying or not. You are responsible for their safety and liable for any injuries they might sustain. If in doubt, declare an emergency. If you do find yourself in real difficulty, waste no time in requesting assistance from ATC or on the appropriate CTAF or UNICOM frequency. Timely action may avoid an even more serious emergency.

What Is Considered To Be an Emergency?

It is impossible to outline all possible emergency situations. The declaration of an emergency by the pilot in command is a matter of operational judgment. Emergencies can be classified according to the urgency and to the degree of seriousness of the consequences—as pilot in command, you decide, but you must always err on the safe side. Some categories might be:

- uncertainty of position and inability to confirm direction to proceed;
- uncertainty of position and fuel reserves;
- loss of oil pressure, a rough running engine, or fuel depletion that may be insufficient to reach an airport;
- some doubt about the serviceability of the airplane or systems or the medical condition of the pilot;
- loss of electrical power;
- loss of the primary attitude indicator; and
- risk of loss of control because of reduced visibility or risk of controlled flight into terrain because of rising ground and lowering cloud base.

It is impossible to set hard and fast rules. If in doubt, tell someone what the potential problem is and do it earlier rather than later—when there is still plenty of time and fuel. If there is any urgency, formally declare an emergency—at least a pan-pan. If there is any risk of loss of control or injury, declare a mayday.

To Declare an Emergency

If an emergency arises, it is your responsibility as pilot in command to assess just how serious the emergency is (or could be) and to take appropriate safety action. The pilot has the ultimate responsibility for the safety of the airplane.

Many emergencies require your immediate attention and occupy you fully for some moments, but it is advisable at the first opportune moment to tell someone. Radio can play a vital role when assistance is required; however, in an emergency, always remember that your first priority is to control and position the airplane.

There are two degrees of emergency; as pilot in command, you should preface your radio call with either:
- *mayday* (repeated three times) for a *distress* call; or
- *pan-pan* (repeated three times) for an *urgency* call.

Distress Message (Mayday Call)

A mayday is the absolute top priority call. It has priority over all others, and the word *mayday* should force everyone else into immediate radio silence (mayday is the anglicized spelling of the French *m'aidez!* [help me]). You should make a distress call as soon as is convenient following the onset of the emergency. You must use your operational judgment, and you must not delay transmission of the distress message (e.g. by trying to determine your position precisely in the absence of suitable landmarks or in conditions of poor visibility).

When you require immediate assistance and are being threatened by grave and immediate danger, the mayday distress message should be transmitted over the air-ground frequency you are presently using.

If there is no response—and if time permits—change frequency to 121.5 MHz (the international emergency frequency usually monitored by airliners and some ground stations), and repeat your distress call.

If your airplane is transponder equipped, squawk code 7700 (the emergency and urgency transponder code). If you are in a radar environment, this causes a special symbol to appear around your airplane on the ATC radar screen and rings an alarm bell immediately alerting the ATC radar controllers.

For example, you experience an emergency in the Gilldoola area and transmit your distress call on the local frequency (on which you are maintaining a listening watch).

Pilot: *Mayday mayday mayday*
Foxtrot Papa Delta, Foxtrot Papa Delta, Foxtrot Papa Delta
two zero miles west of Gilldoola at this time
altitude four thousand
White Cessna one eight two with red stripes
engine failure
forced landing in open paddock
one person on board.

There is no reference to heading, airspeed, or endurance in this call, as the pilot considers them to be irrelevant.

Air traffic control would acknowledge this call as follows:

ATC: *Foxtrot Papa Delta*
        Brisbane
        Roger mayday
        Do you require assistance?

Appropriate search and rescue (SAR) action would then be commenced under the supervision of the senior air traffic controller. The SAR action may include Brisbane air traffic control imposing radio silence on all other traffic, if appropriate.

If there is no immediate response from a ground station acknowledging your call, the distress message should be repeated at intervals. Other airplanes hearing the mayday call will have imposed radio silence on themselves, but having noted that the distress call was not acknowledged by a ground station, they may at this stage be able to assist by relaying the distress call to a ground station.

Urgency Message (Pan-Pan Call)

When an emergency exists but does not require immediate assistance, an urgency or pan-pan message is made over the frequency in use. Typical situations in which a pan-pan urgency message is appropriate include the following:

- if you are experiencing navigational difficulties and require the urgent assistance of air traffic control;
- if you have a passenger on board who requires urgent medical attention;
- if the safety of an airplane or a ship you observe is threatened and urgent action is perhaps needed; and
- if you are making an emergency change of level in controlled airspace and you may conflict with traffic below.

For example:

Pilot: *Pan-pan pan-pan pan-pan*
          Adelaide
          Alfa Charlie Echo
          two zero miles south of Broken Hill at three zero
          heading two five zero
          airspeed nine zero knots
          three thousand feet
          Piper Warrior
          experiencing severely reduced visibility in dust storm
          descending to land on agricultural strip.

Priority of Calls

Of the two emergency calls, the distress call has top priority. The urgency call does not have as high a priority as the mayday. Other pilots should impose radio silence for a suitable period depending on the circumstances. *Any airplane in an emergency situation has priority over all other airplanes.*

If a situation giving rise to a mayday or pan-pan call changes so that the distress or urgency condition no longer exists, the pilot should cancel the call by transmitting "cancel mayday" or "cancel pan-pan" and cease squawking code 7700 on the transponder.

Imposition of Radio Silence

An airplane in distress or the appropriate ground station can impose radio silence on all other stations in the area or on any station causing interference by asking them to stop transmitting:

> Pilot: *All stations*
> *silence* (pronounced *"SEE-lance"*)
> *mayday.*

Loss of Radio Communication

Loss of communication can cause problems in flight, especially when operating in busy terminal areas. The AIM gives guidance on the procedures to follow in the event of loss of radio (refer to figure 7-2, page 138). If radio failure occurs in flight, you should try to locate and rectify the fault (your flight instructor will show you the routine fault-finding procedure for your airplane). It will involve a procedure of checking the items as outlined below.

Failure to Establish or Maintain Communication

Air to Ground

If you are unable to communicate with a ground station on the desired frequency, there could be a total loss of communication. Alternatively, you might hear the ground station without the ground station hearing you (or vice versa). Check the following:
- correct frequency selection;
- sidetone;
- headset plugged in correctly;
- airplane master/avionics switch on, NAV/COM set on and volume correctly set;
- squelch function and level;
- speaker/headphones correctly selected or audio selector panel (if installed) correctly set (try using the hand-held microphone in the case of headset failure or vice versa); and
- circuit breakers/fuses, but only if easily accessible without distraction to normal flight.

If you still have no success, try communicating on an alternate frequency if available, or revert to the previous frequency in use. Otherwise, consider requesting another airplane to relay your message, or try any other ground station.

4-2-13. Communications with Tower when Aircraft Transmitter or Receiver or Both are Inoperative

a. Arriving Aircraft.

1. Receiver inoperative.

(a) If you have reason to believe your receiver is inoperative, remain outside or above the Class D surface area until the direction and flow of traffic has been determined; then, advise the tower of your type [of] aircraft, position, altitude, intention to land, and request that you be controlled with light signals.

REFERENCE-
AIM, Traffic Control Light Signals, Paragraph 4-3-13.

(b) When you are approximately 3 to 5 miles from the airport, advise the tower of your position and join the airport traffic pattern. From this point on, watch the tower for light signals. Thereafter, if a complete pattern is made, transmit your position downwind and/or turning base leg.

2. Transmitter inoperative. Remain outside or above the Class D surface area until the direction and flow of traffic has been determined; then, join the airport traffic pattern. Monitor the primary local control frequency as depicted on Sectional Charts for landing or traffic information, and look for a light signal which may be addressed to your aircraft. During hours of daylight, acknowledge tower transmissions or light signals by rocking your wings. At night, acknowledge by blinking the landing or navigation lights. To acknowledge tower transmissions during daylight hours, hovering helicopters will turn in the direction of the controlling facility and flash the landing light. While in flight, helicopters should show their acknowledgement of receiving a transmission by making shallow banks in opposite directions. At night, helicopters will acknowledge receipt of transmissions by flashing either the landing or the search light.

3. Transmitter and receiver inoperative. Remain outside or above the Class D surface area until the direction and flow of traffic has been determined; then, join the airport traffic pattern and maintain visual contact with the tower to receive light signals. Acknowledge light signals as noted above.

b. Departing Aircraft. If you experience radio failure prior to leaving the parking area, make every effort to have the equipment repaired. If you are unable to have the malfunction repaired, call the tower by telephone and request authorization to depart without two-way radio communications. If tower authorization is granted, you will be given departure information and requested to monitor the tower frequency or watch for light signals as appropriate. During daylight hours, acknowledge tower transmissions or light signals by moving the ailerons or rudder. At night, acknowledge by blinking the landing or navigation lights. If radio malfunction occurs after departing the parking area, watch the tower for light signals or monitor tower frequency.

REFERENCE-
14 CFR Section 91.125 and 14 CFR Section 91.129.

Figure 7-2 Extract from AIM (para. 4-2-13).

If operating in a radar environment and you lose radio contact, squawk 7600 on your transponder. Stay in VMC and land at the most suitable airport. Follow AIM procedures in controlled airspace.

Following a Loss of Communications Should You Land As Soon As Possible?

After experiencing a radio failure, your operational judgment will determine what procedures you follow and whether you land at the nearest suitable airport or complete the flight planned route. *Do not allow the radio failure to unsettle you. The airplane does not need a radio to fly!*

ATC Light Signals

Unless otherwise authorized, aircraft are required to maintain two-way radio communication with the airport control towers when operating to, from, or on the controlled airport, regardless of the weather. If radio contact cannot be maintained, ATC will direct traffic by means of light gun signals. By day, tower transmissions or light signals are acknowledged by moving the ailerons or rudder. At night, tower transmissions or light signals are acknowledged by blinking the landing or navigation lights. If you experience a radio failure once you have departed the parking area, you need to watch the tower for light signals or monitor the tower frequency. Between sunset and sunrise, a pilot wishing to attract the attention of the control tower should turn on a landing light and taxi the aircraft into a position clear of the active runway so that light is visible to the tower. The landing light should remain on until appropriate signals are received from the tower.

If the aircraft radios fail while inbound to a tower-controlled airport, the pilot should remain outside or above the airport traffic area until the direction and flow of traffic have been determined and then join the airport traffic pattern and watch the tower for light signals.

The general warning signal (alternating red and green) may be followed by any other signal. For example, while on final approach for landing, an alternating red and green light followed by a flashing red light is received from the control tower. Under these circumstances, the pilot should abandon the approach, realizing the airport is unsafe for landing.

Light Signal	Meaning in Flight	Meaning on Ground
Steady Green	Cleared to land if pilot satisfied no collision risk exists.	Cleared to takeoff if pilot satisfied no collision risk exists.
Steady Red	Give way to other aircraft and continue circling.	Stop.
Green Flashes	Return for landing.	Cleared to taxi if pilot satisfied no collision risk exists.
Red Flashes	Airport unsafe—do not land.	Taxi clear of landing area in use.
White Flashes	No significance.	Return to starting point on airport.

Table 7-1 Light signals used to control airplanes.

Emergency Locator Transmitter (ELT)

The emergency locator transmitter (also known as the *VHF survival beacon* (VSB) and *emergency locator beacon* (ELB)) is a VHF radio transmitter capable of sending a signal simultaneously on the international distress frequencies of 121.5 and 243 MHz when activated. Each unit has its own power source (battery), so before setting out on a flight where the carriage of an ELT is required, *check that the battery recharge date (stamped on the ELT) has not expired.*

ELTs can easily be activated unintentionally, possibly causing unnecessary rescue action. As a check, it is a good idea to monitor the radio briefly on 121.5 MHz prior to leaving the taxiing area at the commencement of a flight and when taxiing back to the parking area at the completion of the flight. If an ELT signal is detected, check the status of your own ELT. If the signal is from another ELT, report reception of the signal to the nearest air traffic facility (refer to figure 7–3).

6-2-5. Emergency Locator Transmitter (ELT)

d. Inflight Monitoring and Reporting.

1. Pilots are encouraged to monitor 121.5 MHz and/or 243.0 MHz while inflight to assist in identifying possible emergency ELT transmissions. On receiving a signal, report the following information to the nearest air traffic facility:

(a) Your position at the time the signal was first heard.

(b) Your position at the time the signal was last heard.

(c) Your position at maximum signal strength.

(d) Your flight altitudes and frequency on which the emergency signal was heard: 121.5 MHz or 243.0 MHz. If possible, positions should be given relative to a navigation aid. If the aircraft has homing equipment, provide the bearing to the emergency signal with each reported position.

Figure 7-3 Extract from AIM (para. 6-2-5 (d)).

Action by Airplanes Hearing an ELT Signal

Airplanes equipped to receive on emergency frequencies 121.5 or 243 MHz should monitor these frequencies and, if convenient, report any signals heard (ELTs emit a siren–type sound). Report the reception to the nearest air traffic facility.

Engine Problems

Engine Symptoms

It is usual to hear slight changes in the engine note when you fly cross-country at night, enter cloud or rain, fly over mountains, or fly overwater. Most changes may be imaginary, but not all. In cloud, there can be changes in engine note or airflow noise because of rain, hail, turbulence, or icing. Watch the rpm and oil pressure. If there is any rpm drop or fluctuation, select carburetor heat to hot. If there is any oil pressure drop, declare a pan-pan, and plan the safest route to descend if it becomes inevitable. Consider a diversion to the nearest safe airport. If there are any fuel pressure fluctuations or rough running, change tanks, select "both," turn on the boost pump, and check the mixture—it could be too rich or too lean. Check that the primer is in and locked—if it is creeping out, it will cause rough running.

Engine Failure: Single Engine

Takeoff

On the runway, an aborted takeoff is the same at night as during the day. After liftoff, set the glide attitude, gear down, full flaps, landing light on, and look for any clear path. Do not even consider a turn back unless you are established in the climb and you can see the runway through the windshield or side windows.

Cruise

Total engine failure at night is a crisis, and the prospect of a forced landing at night is probably the single most common reason why many pilots avoid night flight. Again, the answer lies in the planning and route selection. Do not forget you will also lose the vacuum (suction) system with engine failure if your airplane has an engine-driven vacuum pump. Electrical services and avionics are restricted by the capacity and condition of the battery.

Set the glide attitude and airspeed, and trim the airplane. Carry out the immediate actions and trouble checks. The likely causes are fuel (contents, selection, pump, or mixture) or carburetor icing, and these may be easily corrected.

There are few cues to locate a suitable landing area. If you have planned the flight, it may be that you can detect a beach or lake shore. Turn to an airport on your flight path if possible. Conserve electrical power. Turn off everything except one radio and the cockpit lights. Save battery power for a mayday call and brief illumination of the landing light for touchdown. Do not believe the vacuum instruments. Turn toward any lit area that provides an attitude reference. A highway may be the only option, but there may be power lines, which are almost impossible to see at night. Be wary of high terrain and note the local elevation. Wind is a consideration; if you have a choice, land into the wind. A forested area may be acceptable if the trees are small and you settle gently and slowly into the tree tops. An upslope is a better option than down, and it will show better in the landing light. You will need to flare earlier and more. Land level and in control, avoiding the stall/spin scenario.

If over water, be especially diligent about altitude. Over glassy smooth water, or at night without sufficient light, it is very easy for even the most experienced pilots to misjudge altitude by 50 feet or more. A slightly greater than normal approach speed should be used down to the flare-out.

Approach and Landing

A night approach and pattern entry is the same as during the day, so there is not enough altitude to glide to the runway in the event of engine failure after passing abeam the threshold on downwind. Think about this when on base and final. Have a preselected clear area and direction to turn in mind.

Engine Failure at Night

If the engine fails at night, several important procedures and considerations to keep in mind are as follows:

- Maintain positive control of the airplane and establish the best glide configuration and airspeed. Turn the airplane towards an airport or away from congested areas.
- Check to determine the cause of the engine malfunction, such as the position of fuel selectors, magneto switch, or primer. If possible, the cause of the malfunction should be corrected immediately and the engine restarted.
- Announce the emergency situation to air traffic control (ATC) or UNICOM. If already in radio contact with a facility, do not change frequencies, unless instructed to change.
- If the condition of the nearby terrain is known, turn towards an unlighted portion of the area. Plan an emergency approach to an unlighted portion.
- Consider an emergency landing area close to public access if possible. This may facilitate rescue or help, if needed.
- Maintain orientation with the wind to avoid a downwind landing.
- Complete the before landing checklist, check the landing lights for operation at altitude, and turn them on in sufficient time to illuminate the terrain or obstacles along the flight path. The landing should be completed in the normal landing attitude at the slowest possible airspeed. If the landing lights are unusable and outside visual references are not available, the airplane should be held in level-landing attitude until the ground is contacted.
- After landing, turn off all switches and evacuate the aircraft as quickly as possible.

Engine Failure: Twin

Night Takeoff

Have your self-brief before lining up on the runway. Mentally rehearse immediate actions in the event of an engine failure before and after liftoff or gear selection. Plan your actions to return for an engine-out landing—but do not rush. Clean up the airplane and gain altitude before turning.

Cruise

During the cruise, engine failure in a twin is not a major problem. Control the yaw and use the autopilot. Carry out a trouble check—especially of fuel contents and selection. Nurse the live engine by reducing power and opening the cowl flaps. Allow a cruise descent but not below the lowest safe altitude. Change track if there is an option with lower terrain.

Approach and Landing

Engine failure during the approach and landing is quite controllable. Continue to fly the approach while preventing any yaw. Keep the ball centered (which means there is a slight sideslip, but flying wings level with the ball centered is probably less disorienting than banking toward the live engine). During the approach, you need low power, and so performance is probably not an issue. Consider retracting the landing gear until a normal approach path is assured. Do not select full flaps until you have reached the decision height and you have made the decision to continue. Even then, it may be better to continue with partial flaps rather than full—it will depend on the airplane type and the effects of flaps in that airplane.

Electrical System Failure

Unless your airplane has two engines and two alternators, the electrical system has one power source (the alternator) and one short-term backup (the battery). The engine ignition, vacuum-driven instruments, pressure instruments, and flight controls are unaffected in a small airplane, but you may lose some or all of the following:

- autopilot;
- some internal lights and all external lights;
- some instruments (and pitot heat);
- flaps (electric);
- NAVAIDs; and
- radios and intercom.

An electrical failure may compromise the attitude indicator, the heading indicator, or the turn coordinator—but not all three together. It is not permitted for them to share a common power source. Some turn coordinators have an independent power supply. An electrical failure could make the pitot heat unavailable, leading to icing problems. An electrical failure will also cause the radios to eventually fail when the battery energy is consumed. Navigation becomes *dead reckoning* (DR) unless you have a hand-held GPS. Radar assistance may be requested, but that requires radios. Use your mobile phone if necessary.

You may have electrically operated flaps, so a flapless landing may be required. You will lose all but the emergency cockpit lighting. Plan a no-radio pattern entry for a flapless landing with no landing light. It is not as serious as it sounds. You will be able to operate each of these services for a limited time on the battery (hopefully it was fully charged and serviceable). The pitot heat, landing lights, and flaps motor all use significant electrical capacity. Remember that not only can you not see other airplanes, they cannot see you—either visually or via your transponder.

With total electrical failure, *fly the airplane*. Maintain attitude while you get the flashlight set up. Use your copilot to assist, and ensure that he or she keeps the primary flight instruments illuminated. Save what battery life you have for radio calls and a brief use of the landing light by switching off all non-essential electrical services.

You may be able to reselect the alternator after reducing the electrical load or turning off any suspect equipment. Try it once, but only if there is no electrical smell and no signs of electrical short or fire. Remember to fly the airplane, concentrating on your orientation, paperwork, and flashlights. Plan the approach and use the copilot.

If there are indications of an electrical failure, check that the master switch is on, and check any circuit breakers or fuses. Do not interrupt your flight instrument scan for more than a few seconds. (In some airplanes, master switches also act as circuit breakers, particularly the split-rocker type master switches. They can be turned on and off to recycle, an action which may restore full or partial electrical power.)

No-Light Landing

A night landing without the landing light is not difficult. Many pilots make better landings without the light because they are not tempted to fly down the beam, and they take a wider view of the runway perspective. Bear in mind that other airplanes and the tower will not be able to see you. It is your responsibility to look out for them.

Cockpit Lighting Failure

The loss of external lighting is not as serious as the loss of cockpit lighting. All flight is visual—whether it is by reference to the real-world horizon or the miniature one inside the attitude indicator. To retain control, you must be able to see one of these. In this situation, your fully charged, hand-held flashlight will save your life and the lives of your passengers.

Pitot-Static System

Pitot Tube Blockage

A damaged or iced pitot tube may affect the airspeed indicator. It may even freeze totally. The use of electric pitot heat will generally prevent the occurrence of icing problems in the pitot-static system. However, a more serious and embarrassing situation is a pitot cover that has not been removed prior to flight. Check that the ASI reads before liftoff.

If the ASI is unusable in flight, all is not lost. Selecting a suitable attitude on the AI and suitable power on the power indicator should result in the desired performance. Some flight and operations manuals provide tables of power settings and attitudes for use in the event of an ASI failure. If none is available, it is a simple matter to commit the basic settings for the various configurations of flight to memory—you should know them already.

Static Vent Blockage

A damaged or blocked static system will affect the ASI, the altimeter, and the VSI. If totally blocked, a constant static pressure may be trapped in the system. The altimeter indication will not alter, and the VSI will remain on zero, even when the airplane changes altitude. The ASI will indicate an incorrect airspeed. As the airplane climbs, trapped static pressure will cause the ASI to read too low. The danger is to follow the false ASI reading and accelerate, possibly exceeding V_{NE} (never exceed speed).

Conversely, the trapped pressure will cause the ASI to overread on descent. The danger on descent is to follow the false ASI indication and slow up, possibly stalling. Most airplanes are installed with an alternate static source. If this is selected, the affected instruments should become usable, with a need to apply corrections to the indications in some cases.

Remember that cabin pressure in a nonpressurized airplane is slightly lower than the external static pressure because of the venturi effect created by the motion of the airplane through the air. This slightly lower static pressure could cause the altimeter to read 50 feet to 100 feet too high and the airspeed indicator to read 5 knots or so too high. The vertical speed indicator will show a brief climb as the lower static pressure is introduced, but it will then settle down and read accurately.

Failure of Airport Lighting

Most airports have a standby power supply that will operate within seconds of an airport power failure, but there is a possibility that a complete power failure could occur. Airplanes in the vicinity of an airport without runway lighting at night should hold at a safe altitude. If the lighting is not returned to service, consideration should be given to diverting (at a safe altitude) to a nearby airport where runway lighting is available. A radar service may be available to assist in tracking.

Partial-Panel Instrument Flying

Attitude Indicator or Vacuum Failure

Although airplane instrumentation is becoming increasingly more reliable, many GA airplanes are ten, twenty, or even thirty years old, and we have to consider the possibility of one or more instruments failing in flight. The most serious failure is that of the attitude indicator or its power source—a normal scan will show that the AI is not responding or is toppling or that the vacuum gauge is showing a loss of suction. Immediately mistrust the AI and give greater emphasis to the other instruments. The AI may fail totally and suddenly, or it may wander as the gyro slows. In either event, try to ignore it. If you do not have a standby attitude indicator, you are now on *partial (limited)* panel.

On partial panel, you must use second-hand information to deduce the airplane's attitude. It is necessary to treat pitch attitude and bank angle separately. Try not to change both together—have one under control and stabilized before varying the other. Without the AI, the effects of inertia may appear to be more marked—make changes smoothly and gently using the "change, check, hold, adjust, trim" technique. Any tendency to chase the needles must be consciously avoided.

Because of the absence of immediate and direct presentation of attitude changes and because the ASI, altimeter, and VSI suffer lag, it is even more important to hold any new attitude (constant control position) and allow time for the performance instruments to stabilize before making any further adjustments. Then trim.

In a partial-panel situation, reduce the rate and extent of control movement and pause between inputs. The lag in readings will then be less severe, and there will be less tendency to over-control. Small control inputs should be made then the controls checked and held while the performance instruments catch up and settle into their new readings. Fine-tune with further adjustments before trimming.

When using a partial panel, the scan will need to be modified to bypass the unusable instruments. A toppled AI can be very distracting because you have learned to trust it. Cover it if necessary. Focus on the instruments that will give you the information you require. Refer to the turn coordinator for bank—it will not tell you the bank angle directly, but it will tell you if the airplane is yawing or rolling and, if it is, which way and at what rate; you can get some idea of bank angle from this. Keep the ball centered because the turn coordinator and turn indicator respond to yaw. Center the ball, and then the little airplane or turn needle can be centered (rolled) to level the wings.

The autopilot often has its own source of attitude information (e.g. from the turn coordinator) if the AI is vacuum-driven. It can be of great assistance if the vacuum system or AI fails. For pitch attitude, you need to leave the power constant and use the ASI, altimeter, and VSI as guides to level flight. The position of the control column is an important cue to attitude in relation to airspeed—control column back, high attitude, low airspeed; control column a little forward, attitude reduced, airspeed increased.

For wings level or for a standard-rate turn (do not use more than standard rate), the turn coordinator is the vital cue. The airplane is then controlled by two separate interpretations and actions—pitch and roll (bank). It is vital to level the wings and keep them level. The turn coordinator will lag, and so to straighten from a turn, roll toward level and center the ailerons as the needle passes standard rate. Wait a moment and then make a correction. Then, while keeping the wings level, adjust the back pressure to hold a constant airspeed. If the airspeed is increasing, the nose has dropped and vice versa. Apply back pressure until the airspeed stops increasing, and hold (check) that position. Then trim.

Flying on a partial panel is not a precise task, and it is not an easy task unless you are well practiced and have no other workload. Declare an emergency (mayday) and maintain straight and level. If you must turn, tread warily, and do not bank past standard rate.

Interpreting Pitch Attitude on Partial Panel

If the AI is unusable, the pilot can determine the pitch attitude of the airplane by interpreting the indications of the ASI, altimeter, and VSI. The altimeter provides indirect information regarding pitch attitude. For example, if altitude is constant in straight-and-level flight, the pitch attitude is correct for level flight at that power setting, whereas if it is increasing or decreasing, the pitch attitude is too high or too low.

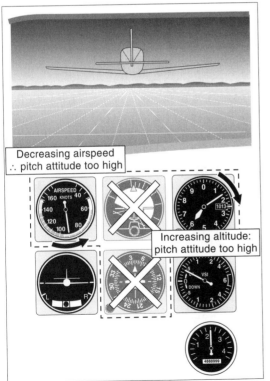
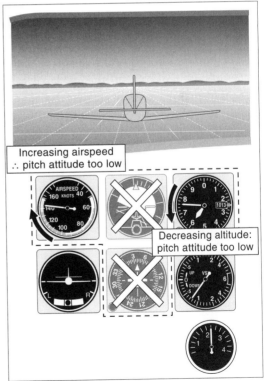

Figure 7-4 (Left) pitch attitude too high; (right) pitch attitude too low.

The ASI also provides pitch attitude information. If the ASI shows that the desired airspeed is being maintained, the pitch attitude is correct for the power set. If it indicates an increasing or higher-than-desired airspeed, the pitch attitude is too low for the power set. Conversely, if the ASI indicates a low or decreasing airspeed, the pitch attitude is too high.

The ASI is an extremely valuable guide to pitch attitude when used in conjunction with the altimeter, but it should be remembered that, because of inertia, an airplane will take some time to change speed. Therefore, the ASI indication must be stabilized before it can be interpreted as an indication of pitch attitude set. In other words, the new attitude must be held for a few seconds to allow the airspeed to settle.

The VSI also provides information about pitch attitude. For example, if the VSI indication remains at zero in straight-and-level flight, the pitch attitude is correct for level flight at that power, whereas a significant and sustained departure from zero on the VSI would indicate a pitch attitude that is either too high or too low.

In a climb or descent, a steady and fairly constant VSI reading will indicate a steady pitch attitude, as will the other performance instruments. Remember that large or sudden changes in pitch attitude will cause the VSI to initially give false readings—another reason to avoid over-controlling when flying on a partial panel. The VSI may read erratically in turbulence, so use it with caution, and even then only when the readings are relatively steady.

Interpreting Bank Attitude on Partial Panel

The pilot can determine bank attitude from the turn coordinator (with the coordination ball centered). The HI (if it is available) and the magnetic compass are also useful as an indirect indication of bank. If the airplane is in coordinated flight (i.e. ball centered), any indication of turning will mean that the airplane is banked. A steady zero rate of turn reading on the turn coordinator with the ball centered will mean that the wings are level. The normal rate of turn is standard rate, which is a rate of change of heading of 3°/second.

Maintaining Control

Keep the wings level. The turn indicator or coordinator becomes the replacement for the AI and must become the focal point of your radial scan. Keep recentering the turn needle or leveling the airplane symbol. While doing this, cross-check the airspeed trend and the altimeter. Make small continuous corrections. Do not let any parameter start to wander.

Entering a Climb

Under some circumstances, it may be safer to climb above a cloud layer than to descend. There may be a later clear area for a visual descent. Seek radar assistance. A climb is entered as for visual flight. Apply climb power slowly and smoothly keeping the ball centered, and allow the nose to rise a little. Keep the wings level. Hold the nose attitude constant as the airspeed decays. Watch the rate of decay as a guide to correct attitude. As the airspeed approaches normal climb speed, hold the control column in a constant position and trim.

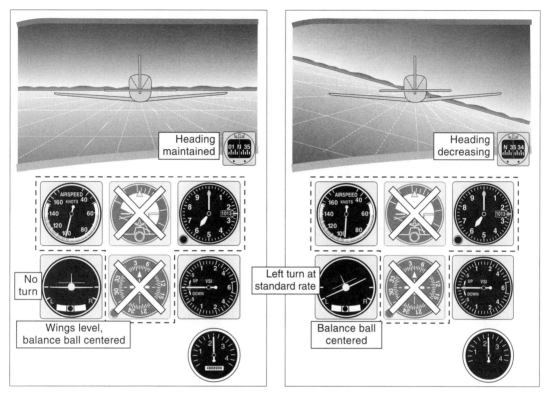

Figure 7-5 Determining bank attitude on partial panel.

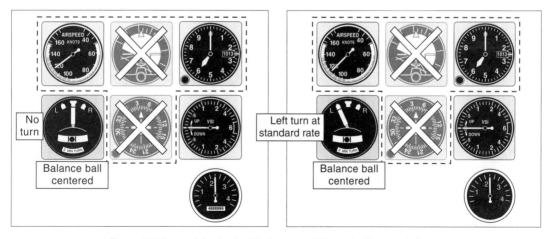

Figure 7-6 Determining bank attitude on a partial panel with a turn indicator.

Entering a Descent

Reduce power a little (not to idle as this will give a very pronounced nose-down pitching and yawing moment). Keep the ball centered and allow the nose to drop a little. Then hold the control column fixed. Watch the airspeed trend and adjust the control position.

Entering a Turn

Do not consider turning unless the airplane is stabilized and trimmed in straight and controlled flight. Gently roll into the turn, and maintain slight back pressure as you roll. Watch the airspeed, but, importantly, do not allow the bank to continue past standard rate. If the airspeed starts to increase, roll back to wings level, adjust the attitude and start again.

Descending and Turning

Unless you are experienced, a combined turn and descent carries potential risk, as there will be a tendency to overbank and for the nose to drop. Stop the bank and watch the airspeed. Any increase that is not immediately corrected should trigger a return to wings level and then to level flight.

Timed Turns

Timed turns are a last resort. The standard rate is 3°/second. The most important numbers are 180° in 60 seconds and 90° in 30 seconds. Do not focus too much on the clock. Note the time starting and count to yourself while flying the airplane. When you are close to the desired time, check the clock and start to roll out. The time should be taken from the start of rolling in to the start of rolling out. When steady, check the magnetic compass and make a correction.

On full panel, the angle of bank to turn at standard rate depends on the true airspeed—the higher the true airspeed, the larger the angle of bank required. A rough guide which assumes IAS is the same as TAS is that bank angle will be equal to airspeed divided by 10 plus 7. For example, the angle of bank required to maintain standard rate at 100 knots is $100 \div 10 + 7 = 17°$.

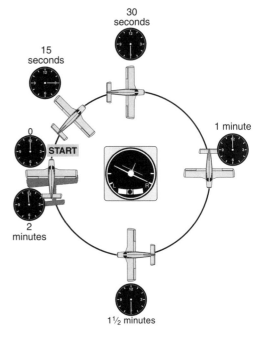

Figure 7-7 Standard-rate turn.

Unusual Attitude Recoveries: Full Panel

An unusual attitude is an excessively high or low pitch attitude and/or bank angle that, if uncorrected, leads to large and rapid changes in altitude and airspeed.

Unusual attitudes are characterized as:

- a bank in excess of 45°;
- a nose-high attitude with a rapidly decreasing airspeed; and/or
- a nose-low attitude with a rapidly increasing airspeed.

Unusual attitudes are potentially hazardous without a visual horizon, so you should practice the recoveries in the clear.

How Can it Happen?

An unusual attitude may result from an external influence (e.g. turbulence), a mechanical problem (e.g. autopilot or lighting failure), or it can be induced by human factors. For instance, if a pilot becomes disoriented or confused ("Where am I?," "Which way is up?") or is preoccupied with other cockpit duties at the expense of an adequate scan and the bank increases, the nose will drop, and the natural stability of the airplane will cause an increasing speed, bank, and nose-down attitude. The airplane will exceed V_{NE} and will probably suffer structural failure in the process.

Nose-high unusual attitudes are less common, because the pilot can simply let go of the controls, and the airplane will soon be in a nose-low unusual attitude.

The most difficult situations include when full power has been applied for a go-around and the pilot does not check the nose-up pitch (trim change), or when in the first turn after a night takeoff and the pilot is turning and looking over his or her shoulder at the runway.

A mechanical failure can also be the reason for an unusual attitude—for example, an attitude indicator that, unbeknown to the pilot, has either failed completely or is giving false attitude indications. Runaway electric trim can also be a problem in some airplane types.

Whatever the cause of an unusual attitude, the immediate problem is to recognize exactly what the airplane is doing. It is then a matter of safely returning the airplane to a normal flight attitude (generally straight and level). After the recovery, you should determine the cause of the event so as to prevent any recurrence. In unusual attitudes, the physiological sensations may be disconcerting, but do not allow these to influence either the recognition of the attitude or the subsequent recovery action.

Recognizing an Unusual Attitude

If you notice any unusual instrument indications or an unexpected change of performance, or if you experience g-forces or air noise, assume that the airplane is in (or about to enter) an unusual attitude. Increase the scan rate, and determine the actual attitude and/or whether or not an instrument has malfunctioned.

Having Recognized an Unusual Attitude, Do Not Overcontrol

It is easy to overreact to an unusual attitude with rapid and excessive control inputs because the occurrence is so unexpected. The simple message is *don't*! Overreaction can only worsen the situation and possibly lead you to overstressing the airplane or overrevving the engine. When considering recovery techniques, there are two simple principles to keep in mind:

- removal of bank will aid propeller control; and
- intelligent use of power (and drag in some airplanes) will help with controlling airspeed.

Nose-Low Attitude and Increasing Airspeed

Refer to figure 7-9.

Indications

A nose-low unusual attitude will be indicated by a nose-low pitch attitude on the AI with the altimeter unwinding, a high rate of descent on the VSI and increasing airspeed.

An excessive bank angle will often lead to a nose-low attitude, since the nose tends to drop naturally when the wings are banked. If unchecked, this will result in a spiral dive (figure 7-8).

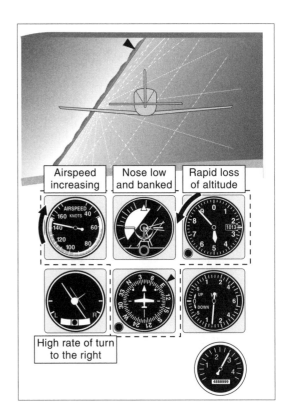

Figure 7-8 Spiral dive.

Recovery

To reduce the rate of airspeed increase and to avoid unnecessary loss of altitude, reduce power—even closing the throttle if necessary. Engine overspeed is possible if this is not done soon enough.

Throttling back and rolling the wings level can be done simultaneously keeping the ball centered, but do not apply back pressure until the wings are level. To ease the airplane out of the dive, smoothly raise the nose through to the level flight position on the attitude indicator.

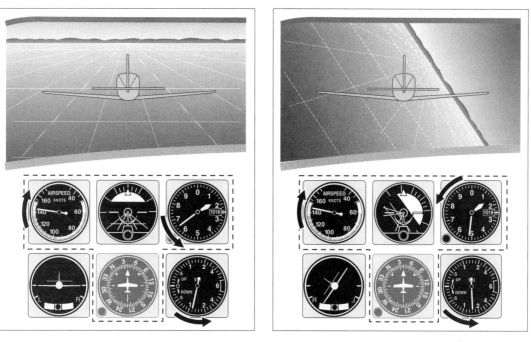

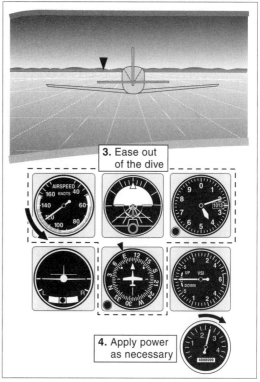

Figure 7-9 Nose-low unusual attitudes (top), and regaining normal flight using the full panel.

If the control column is simply pulled back to raise the nose while the airplane is still steeply banked, the spiral dive will tighten. Therefore, it is most important to roll the wings level first using the AI and the turn coordinator before easing the airplane out of the dive.

There is always a danger of overstressing the airframe with large and sudden control inputs at high airspeeds, particularly if back pressure is applied while the ailerons are deflected. Hence it is necessary to ease the airplane out of the dive with controlled elevator pressure rather than with sudden and panicky movements after rolling wings level.

As the airplane reaches the horizon and the approximate straight-and-level attitude is pegged, the airspeed will "check" (pause momentarily) and then start to decrease. This checking of the indicated airspeed is always a good sign that the horizon has been reached.

The altimeter and VSI readings will also stabilize (subject of course to the considerable lag in the case of the VSI) to indicate level flight or a manageable climb or descent, depending on how accurately the horizon has been pegged. From this point in the recovery, power can be introduced, attitude can be adjusted, and the airplane can be trimmed for straight-and-level flight. Alternatively, if you prefer, you can climb to regain lost altitude.

When in steady straight flight, the heading indicator should be checked to ensure that it is aligned with the magnetic compass.

Nose-High Attitude

Refer to figure 7-10.

Indications

A nose-high unusual attitude will be indicated by the AI, with the altimeter and VSI indicating a climb and decreasing airspeed (possibly rapid). An extremely nose-high attitude might result in the airplane stalling, i.e. the altimeter and VSI suddenly indicating a descent with the airspeed low.

Recovery

When the airplane is in a nose-high/reducing airspeed situation (but not in or near a stall), the recovery involves simultaneously applying full power, lowering the nose, and rolling the wings level with coordinated use of aileron and rudder. The level-flight attitude will be confirmed by the fact that the airspeed change is checked (i.e. it stops decreasing). Having regained normal steady straight flight, you may need to realign the heading indicator.

It is important to note that the initial actions required to recover from an unusual attitude differ according to whether the nose is high or low:

• for a nose-high attitude, you must lower the nose first then level the wings; and
• for a nose-low attitude, you must level the wings first then raise the nose.

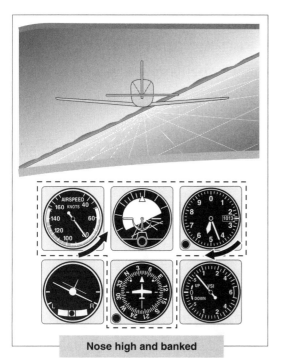

Nose high and banked

Nose high and stalled

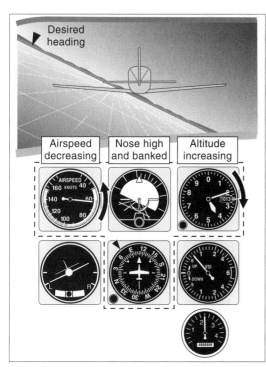

Desired heading

Airspeed decreasing | Nose high and banked | Altitude increasing

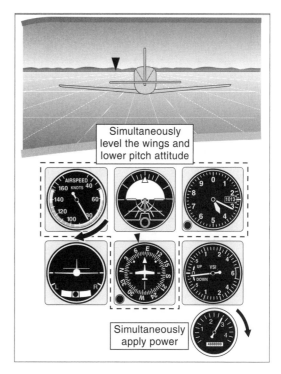

Simultaneously level the wings and lower pitch attitude

Simultaneously apply power

Figure 7-10 Nose-high unusual attitudes (top), and regaining normal flight using the full panel.

Unusual Attitude Recoveries on Partial Panel

In recognizing an unusual attitude, the key points to establish are the following:
• Is the airplane nose high or nose low?
• Is the airplane banked?

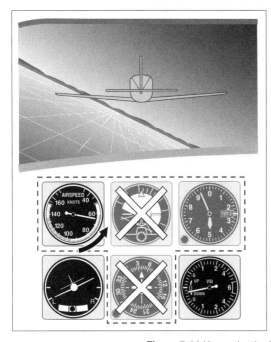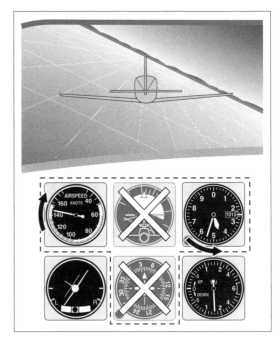

Figure 7-11 Unusual attitudes indicated by a partial panel.

Nose-Low Attitude

Indications

The primary indication of a nose-low attitude will be an increasing airspeed. In addition, the altimeter and VSI will show a high and possibly increasing rate of descent, with bank (if any) confirmed by the turn coordinator.

Recovery

The recovery from a nose-low attitude is the same as for full panel, the only difference being there are fewer instruments available from which to derive information. To recover on a partial panel, the procedure is as follows:
• reduce power;
• reduce any g;
• level the wings using the turn coordinator; and
• ease out of the dive (the horizon is indicated when the airspeed checks and then the altimeter stabilizes).

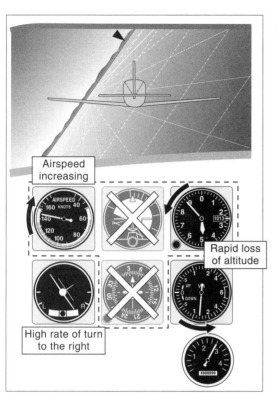

Figure 7-12
(Left) Establish the situation.

Airspeed increasing

Rapid loss of altitude

High rate of turn to the right

Figure 7-13
(Below) Recovery from nose-low and nose-high airspeed on a partial panel.

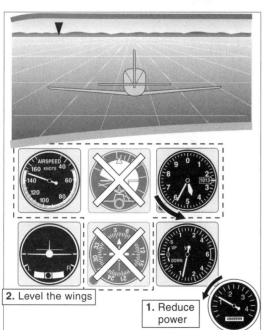

2. Level the wings

1. Reduce power

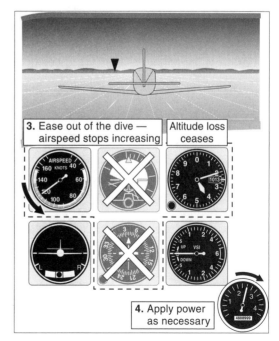

3. Ease out of the dive — airspeed stops increasing

Altitude loss ceases

4. Apply power as necessary

Nose-High Attitude

Indications

If only a partial panel is available, the indications of a nose-high attitude will be as follows:

- a decreasing airspeed on the ASI with supporting information from the altimeter and VSI; and
- bank (if any) indicated on the turn coordinator.

Recovery

Recovery is the same as for a full panel but with the horizon indicated on the ASI when the airspeed is checked and stops decreasing and the altimeter stabilizes. The wings–level bank attitude is achieved when the wings are level on the turn coordinator and the ball is centered.

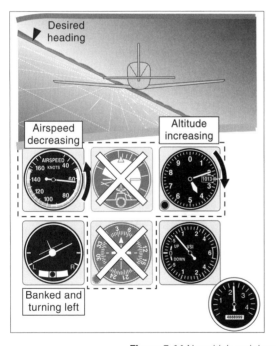 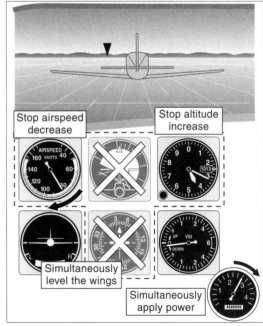

Figure 7-14 Nose high and decreasing airspeed on partial panel.

Part 4

Night Flight Planning and Navigation

Chapter 8

Planning a Night Flight

This chapter is designed to show the step-by-step process of planning a night flight. The procedures and considerations you need to take into account when flying at night are outlined in order to demonstrate the process. The example used for this is an Australian flight from Wagga Wagga to Canberra.

Planning a Night Flight from Wagga Wagga to Canberra

Considerations

We are using a Beech A36 Bonanza with an autopilot and a standby attitude indicator—this airplane complies with the night VFR equipment criteria. We are carrying passengers and therefore need to meet the recency requirements. Fuel is adequate, and loading is within limits. Runways are adequate, and the destination has lighting, emergency power, and an aid. No alternate is required, but we have sufficient fuel to return to Wagga Wagga from Yass if the weather turns.

The FAA offers these tips in planning a night operation:

- Night flying requires that pilots be aware of, and operate within, their abilities and limitations. Although careful planning of any flight is essential, night flying demands more attention to the details of preflight preparation and planning.
- Preparation for a night flight should include a thorough review of the available weather reports and forecasts with particular attention given to temperature/dew-point spread. A narrow temperature/dewpoint spread may indicate the possibility of ground fog, as well as increase the likelihood of carburetor icing. Emphasis should also be placed on wind direction and speed, since the effect of wind on the airplane cannot be as easily detected at night as during the day.
- On night cross-country flights, appropriate aeronautical charts should be selected, including the appropriate adjacent charts. Course lines should be drawn in black to be more distinguishable. File a flight plan!
- Thoroughly review the A/FD for your departure, destination, and alternate airports so you are familiar with which facilities are open and closed during night hours. Keep in mind fuel, restaurants, bathrooms, weather reporting services, and control towers may not be available.
- Prominently lighted checkpoints along the prepared course should be noted. Rotating beacons at airports, lighted obstructions, lights of cities or towns, and lights from major

highway traffic all provide excellent visual checkpoints. The use of NAVAIDs and communication facilities add significantly to the safety and efficiency of night flying.

- All personal equipment should be checked prior to flight to ensure proper functioning. It is very disconcerting to find at a time of need that a flashlight, for example, does not work.
- All airplane lights should be turned on momentarily and checked for operation. Position lights can be checked for loose connections by tapping the light fixture. If the lights blink while being tapped, further investigation to determine the cause should be made prior to flight.
- The parking ramp should be examined prior to entering the airplane. During the day, it is quite easy to see stepladders, chuckholes, wheel chocks, and other obstructions, but at night it is more difficult. A check of the area can prevent taxiing mishaps.

Route Selection

Many factors need to be taken into consideration when deciding which route to choose. Select the route with as many airports, lit obstructions, and cities and towns along the path as possible. Not only do airports aid with pilotage, but they also provide a critical resource in the event of an engine failure. Lit obstructions and light patterns make good checkpoints along your route.

Two choices are available to us when considering which path to fly. The direct route Wagga Wagga—Canberra (WG—CB) is 86 NM measured from the WAC, compared to Wagga Wagga—Yass—Canberra (WG—YASS—CB), the slightly longer route of 104 NM.

Why have two options? Why not take the direct route? When choosing your route, the quickest is often not the safest; in this case, the quickest route offers higher terrain and poor navigation features (two things you do not need at night!).

Calculation of End of Daylight

Prior to deciding which route to take, the calculation of last light needs to be made in order to determine if the flight is to be conducted entirely in darkness. We plan to depart Wagga Wagga at 1830 hours on 30 June. Reference the sunset and sunrise times, available from the National Weather Service or the American Air Almanac (available online at: http://aa.usno.navy.mil) to determine first and last light.

Weather

For this example, the weather is suitable for night VFR as we can maintain the lowest safe altitude clear of cloud. There is a typical thirty-knot wind from the northwest at cruising altitude. There is a likelihood of moderate mechanical turbulence. A cold front is moving in from the southwest with an associated wind change. It is not due until well after our departure, but it may preclude a return to Wagga Wagga if Canberra closes.

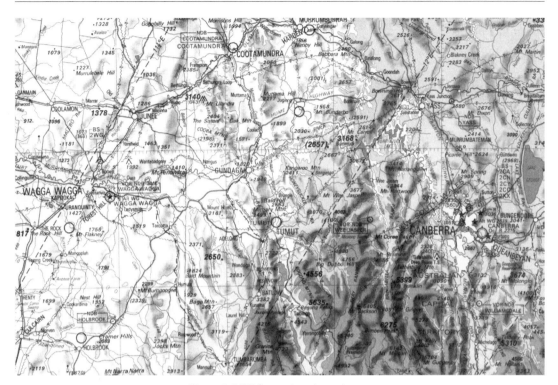

Figure 8-1 WAC covering planned route.

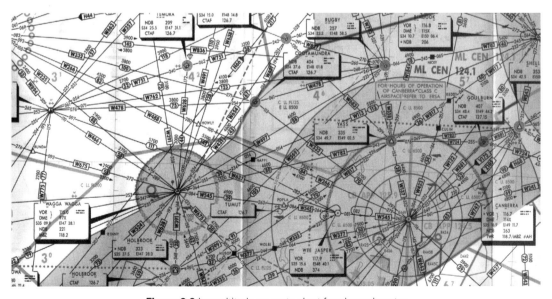

Figure 8-2 Low altitude en route chart for planned sector.

Moon

There is a full moon, so water features—such as the Murrumbidgee River and Lake Burrinjuck—should reflect well depending on our relative positions. Lake George may glow in the eastern distance as we head into Canberra.

Terrain

There is high ground on the direct track, and there are patches of high ground to the north and east. The track via Yass offers lower terrain. Because of the strong winds, there is little likelihood of fog, except in river valleys and sheltered lakes. Airframe icing is likely in cloud, and carburetor icing is possible throughout.

Forced Landing Areas

The direct track passes over Tumut, which offers a useful alternate and forced landing ground. However, the high terrain elsewhere on the direct track is somewhat deterring. There are better forced-landing options in the area of lower terrain on the track via Yass, but it would be a matter of luck to find one in the event of a total engine failure at night. Lit sections of the Hume Highway may offer a survivable outcome, even if the airplane were landed adjacent to the highway.

Navigation Features

The highway from Wagga Wagga to Gundagai to Yass and Yass to Canberra is busy and well lit near towns and major intersections. This offers good night navigation features as it will be clearly visible from the sky. The Burrinjuck Reservoir, as mentioned, should reflect well with the full moon. Yass has an NDB that we can use, although it would be better to turn toward Canberra at Yass township as the NDB takes us over higher terrain.

The direct path does not offer as many navigation features. Initially, the highway will be clear, but as the terrain builds up and Tumut is reached, there are no significant navigation features except for the faint glow of Canberra in the distance and the NDB at Wee Jasper.

There is a lake flying east, so the loss of visual features is earlier than if flying west. There will be no silhouettes of hills, and there will also be no glare from flying into the sunset.

Selection of Cruising Levels

Our flight path is in an easterly direction. When choosing cruising levels, flight must occur at odd thousands plus 500 feet. The lowest safe altitude requirements indicate that you must plan at least 1,000 feet above the highest terrain. To add a further safety margin for night flight, our lowest safe altitude will be 1,500 feet above the highest terrain in a 10 NM direction from track.

In our example, the direct track takes us over higher terrain with a lowest safe altitude of 6,300 feet (from WAC plus 1500 feet). If we plan via Yass, the lowest safe altitude decreases to 4,700 feet and then a further 4,400 feet into Canberra. The lowest cruising levels for the longer route would be 5,500 feet, as compared to 7,500 feet for the direct route.

Visual Features

There will be little to see on the direct track, other than the lights of Tumut and the glow of Canberra as we get closer. These will be obscured by high terrain for most of the flight inbound. If there is a need to turn back, Wagga Wagga offers major lit features. The airfield has a VOR and an NDB. The track via Yass offers a major highway with frequent traffic and lit sections. It promises to be an excellent tracking aid. The choice is to actually follow the highway or to track to the Yass NDB keeping the highway in sight.

Should we track via the YASS NDB? If we pass over the NDB, we are taken well east of the highway to Canberra, and we are placed over higher ground. It appears better to use the aid to track over the township of Yass but then to turn before the NDB and track visually close to the highway inbound to Canberra.

Which Route to Select?

By now the preferred route should be clearly evident. The slightly longer route is often the best, and in this case the situation is true. Wagga Wagga—Yass—Canberra offers better navigational features, lower terrain, and better forced landing areas.

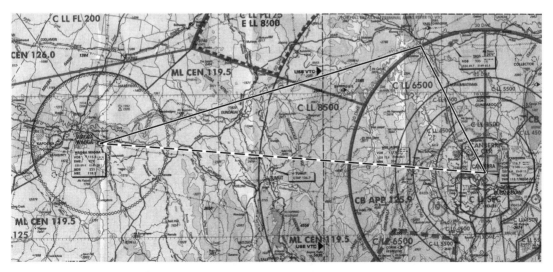

Figure 8-3 Sectional showing route options.

Planning the Fight

Having decided which route to fly, you can now start planning the night flight. There are many factors that need to be taken into consideration, and the planning process is different to day navigation; the light available is limited, and you rely heavily on your preplanning to ensure the workload in the air is minimized. The easiest and simplest way to navigate at night is via a mud map.

What Is a Mud Map?

A true mud map is a thumbnail sketch drawn crudely, but essentially, in sand or mud. The mud eliminates the detail and presents only the essential information. It is difficult to read a chart at night. It is also difficult to find and read information from other data manuals; therefore, the creation of a paper mud map makes night flying much simpler. The mud map assembles important information in an orderly and visible way.

Making a Mud Map

Use a WAC rather than a Sectional, because WACs show topographic features better. Make a double-size photocopy (it becomes 1:500,000 if you zoom to 200%—the same scale as a Sectional), and then make a tracing with the terrain heights. Round up the heights to the next whole hundred feet. From the copy, trace the flight track on a plain sheet of paper.

Use the mud map as your flight plan, and insert all the important information required for the flight, such as the lowest safe altitude, cruising altitude, track, distances, area frequency (obtained from the A/FD), departure and arrival airfield information, and navigation aid information. Highlight all major features that will be easily recognizable from the air, as well as the higher terrain.

Looking at our example, the first step is to draw the flight plan on the WAC and then from there copy the diagram on a plain sheet of paper (figure 8-4).

The mud map should be a simple drawing that highlights only the major features along your track and has all the flight information right in front of you. It is important not to make the mud map too cluttered as you want to be able to see all the information clearly.

When drawing your mud map, write all the names of towns in a black pen with clear writing. Orient the map so that the track is upright. Color should not be used on the map because in a dimly lit cockpit, the rods in our eyes predominate and do not respond to color.

To determine the differences between large towns, small towns, roads, and water features, draw yourself a key and remember it. This allows you to easily identify the differences between features when flying. The key for our mud map is given in figure 8-5 (page 168). For longer routes, make a strip map (concertina folded) and keep the WAC available for diversions.

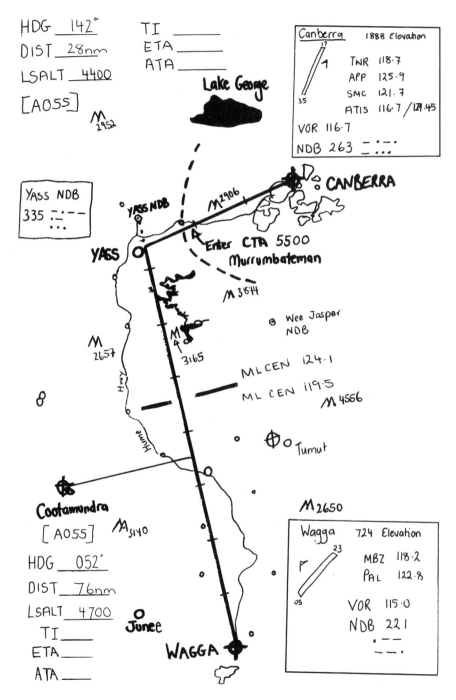

Figure 8-4 Completed mud map (half size).

From the mud map (figure 8-4), you can see that the pilot has all the information required for the flight clearly presented. All the frequencies, navigation aids, airport information, and so on are included on this simple diagram. Although your mud map has all your flight information, always ensure that your navigation items are close to hand (e.g. your charts, A/FD, and computer) as you never know when you may need them. The key is not located on the map—it is the pilot's responsibility to memorize it so that the map is less cluttered. When creating your mud map, spend time on it and do not rush through the planning.

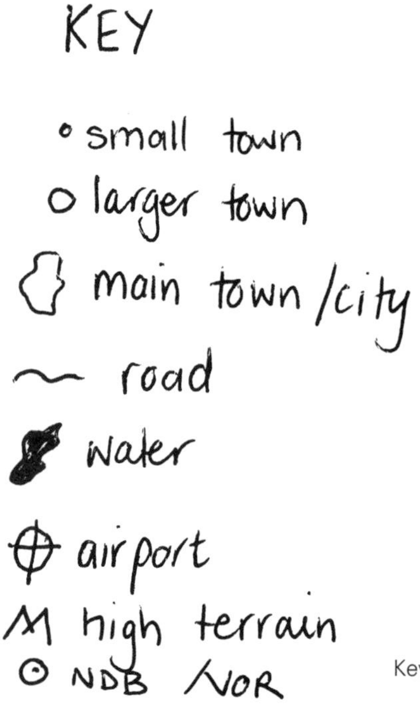

Figure 8-5
Key for the mud map.

The Plan in Detail

Canberra Control

The hours of operation for Canberra control can be found in the Australian equivalent to the U.S. A/FD. Canberra control operates between 0715—2400 hours local (Monday to Friday and Sunday) and 0715—2300 hours local on Saturday. VFR approach points (determined from the Canberra chart) are located at Yass township (at 6,500 feet) or Murrumbateman township (at 5,500 feet), which is on the highway between Yass and Canberra. As our cruising level is 5,500 feet, we will contact Canberra approach from Murrumbateman.

Flight Plan Data

Most of the planning requirements have been taken into consideration, and the mud map has been completed. Therefore, planning a night flight is just like planning any other flight—all the information has been obtained via normal means and can be transferred to the FAA flight plan form.

	Wagga Wagga—Yass	Yass—Canberra
TAS	165 KTAS	165 KTAS
Wind	NW 30 knots	NW 30 knots
Magnetic Variation	12°E	12°E
Heading	052°M	142°M
Track	064°M	154°M
Lowest Safe Altitude	4,700 feet	4,400 feet
Cruising Altitude	5,500 feet	5,500 feet
Frequency	ML CEN 119.5 / 124.1 (from low altitude en route chart)	CB Approach 125.9 Tower 118.7 Ground 121.7 ATIS 127.45
Navigation Aids	Yass NDB 335	VOR 116.7 NDB 263

Table 8-1 Flight plan data.

Escape Routes

Escape routes and *"what ifs"* should always be considered when flying at night, especially in a single-engine airplane. You will notice that one of the considerations in choosing our route to Canberra is the location of possible forced-landing areas. Always have in mind the location of the closest airfield in relation to your position. On a separate sheet of paper in your navigation folder, write out the details of every airfield you will pass or that will be close to track. This way, if you ever need to land because of weather or other circumstances, you have the information readily available to you. Be prepared for a possible lighting failure at your destination airfield, and know the options available—it is recommended that a decision be made before committing to a descent. Plan to carry sufficient fuel to fly to an alternate, even if the weather is alright. Otherwise, calculate a point of no return. This becomes your decision/commitment point.

Point of No Return

The *point of no return* (PNR) is the point beyond which it takes less time and fuel to reach the destination than to return to the departure airfield. The PNR is useful for night cross-country flights—especially in remote areas—as it takes into account the possible situations of the destination airfield not being available and the departure airfield also being the alternate. Sometimes, it is better to return home than to fly to another airfield.

If there is no suitable and closer alternate, the departure airfield is considered suitable for return if the fuel carried is adequate. The PNR is the last point to which the airplane can be flown before the decision is made to continue or return—it is a go/no go point. It is also the point by which the destination weather, lighting, and surface conditions must be confirmed. If there are any doubts, you must turn back.

Calculating PNR

In its simplest form, the location of the PNR can be found by determining the endurance based on the flight fuel available being burned at a constant fuel flow rate:

$$\text{Endurance} = \frac{\text{flight fuel available}}{\text{fuel flow in units per hour}}$$

For example, if we have 70 gallons of flight fuel available and the constant fuel flow rate is 15 gallons per hour, we have:

$$\text{Endurance} = \frac{70 \text{ gallons}}{15 \text{ gallons per hour}}$$

$$\therefore \text{E} = 4.7 \text{ (4 hours and 42 minutes)}$$

PNR is that point beyond which there will be insufficient fuel to return to the departure airfield. With ample fuel, you may reach your destination and still be able to return, i.e. the departure airfield is also an alternate. In our example, we can fly out in still air for 2.35 hours (i.e. half the endurance)—e.g. this will be 360 NM at a TAS of 150 knots. We have used 2.35 hours of our endurance and therefore have E − 2.35 = 2.35 hours available for return. This is the same as our outbound flight.

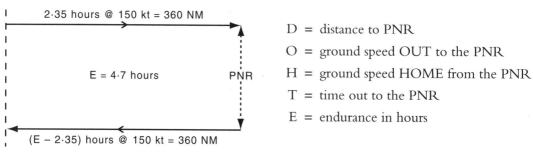

Figure 8-6 Concept of PNR.

Figure 8-7 PNR calculations abbreviations.

If there is a wind blowing, the ground speeds out and home will not be the same. Using our knowledge of the still-air situation, it is easy to develop a formula from which we can find the location of the PNR. Since we know that the distance out to the PNR is equal to the distance home from the PNR, and since distance = time × speed, we can rewrite this as given in figure 8-8.

$$T \times O = (E - T) \times H$$
$$TO = EH - TH$$
$$TO + TH = EH$$
$$T(O + H) = EH$$
$$\therefore \text{ Time to PNR, } T = \frac{EH}{O + H}$$

Figure 8-8 PNR formula.

To calculate the distance out to the PNR:

$$\text{Distance out to PNR } = \frac{EH}{O + H} \text{ (distance)} \times O \text{ (ground speed)}$$
$$\therefore \text{ Distance to PNR, } D = \frac{EOH}{O + H}$$

Recalculating PNR In Flight

PNR calculations are often required in flight. These are made from overhead a positive fix and usually involve the updating of a PNR determined at an earlier stage (e.g. when flight planning prior to departure). However, in-flight PNR calculations may also be required under other circumstances. For example, a flight departs with minimum fuel, based on a lack of operational requirements at the intended destination. However, the pilot is advised en route that the airfield may be closed because of unforecast weather problems. An in-flight PNR calculation is required to determine how much further along track the airplane can proceed—in the hope that the weather will improve—before a diversion back to the departure airfield, or some other suitable alternate, is required.

En route PNR calculations should be tackled in exactly the same way as those involving climbs and descents, i.e. reduce the problem to a simple cruise-only calculation by extracting the flight fuel for all sections of the flight that do not involve cruise out and back.

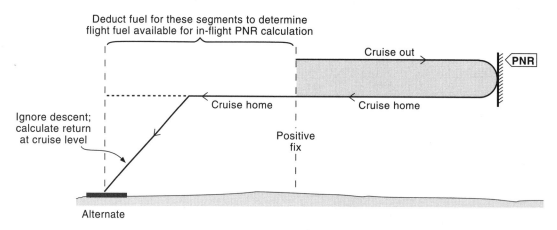

Figure 8-9 In-flight PNR calculations.

Note that the following applies for any in-flight PNR calculation:

- you may ignore the climb segment after departure, as well as all the cruise segment lying behind the airplane;

- a variable reserve is required for the remainder of the flight only, and so the flight fuel available must be recalculated; and

- in-flight winds and fuel flows may often differ from flight plan values (make sure you use the actual figures for wind component, ground speed, and fuel flow to calculate an accurate in-flight PNR).

Chapter 9

Radio Navigation

In some circumstances, navigation may use visual references, but most navigation at night also requires reference to NAVAIDs. In the pattern, the airplane may be *positioned* by reference to the runway or ground features, but it is *flown* by reference to the instruments.

In spite of fewer references or checkpoints, night cross-country flights do not present particular problems if preplanning is adequate, and the pilot continues to monitor position, time estimates, and fuel consumed. Although dead reckoning is possible at night, pilotage will be the more reliable means of navigation. NAVAIDs should be used to assist in monitoring en route progress.

Orientation in Space

The essence of radio navigation is interpreting the information displayed so as to imagine the position of the airplane in space. Two dimensions determine geographic position. The third dimension is displayed on the altimeter. The fourth dimension is displayed on the clock.

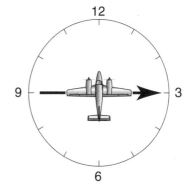

ADF and NDB

The *automatic direction finder* (ADF) needle always points directly to the station and is displayed relative to the top of the instrument (which represents the nose of the airplane). It is exactly the same as the clock-code but more precise. Instead of twelve directions, we can use all 360 and be accurate to one degree. The nose (the top of the instrument) is 12 o'clock or 360°.

The direction of the needle relative to the nose of the airplane is called the *relative bearing* and can be described in one of two ways:

- the number of degrees left or right of the nose (or tail) (e.g. 30° left or 30° right); or
- the number of degrees on the indicator with 360 at the top of the instrument (e.g. 3 o'clock is 090° relative and 9 o'clock is 270° relative).

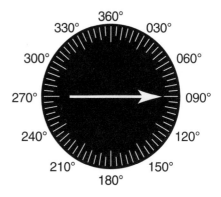

Figure 9-1 Relative bearing is an accurate form of the clock-code.

The use of degrees left or right of the nose removes confusion with magnetic bearings, tracks, and headings.

This relative bearing information is sufficient to find our way to the station (by directly homing), but it does not show where we are—it only shows that the *non-directional beacon* (NDB) is left or right and by how much. We could be anywhere around the circle at any distance. *Note the symbol used for the NDB on the Sectional chart.*

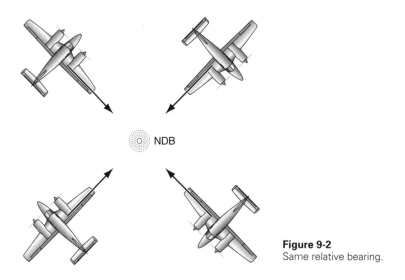

Figure 9-2
Same relative bearing.

If we are to use the NAVAID to find our position, we need a further reference—the heading of the airplane. When this is known, the airplane can only be on one *position line* (but at any distance—as discussed in the following).

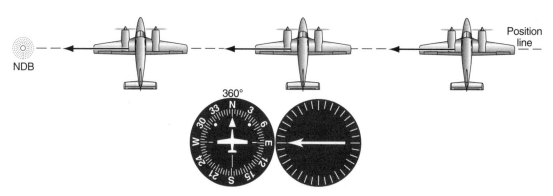

Figure 9-3 The heading and relative bearing provide a position line for the airplane.

In figure 9-4, our heading is 360°M (i.e. relative to magnetic north) and the station is 90° left. Therefore, the *magnetic bearing* (direction or track) *to* the station is 270°, and the magnetic bearing (direction or track) *from* the station to the airplane is the reciprocal of the bearing to the station—in this case, it is 090°.

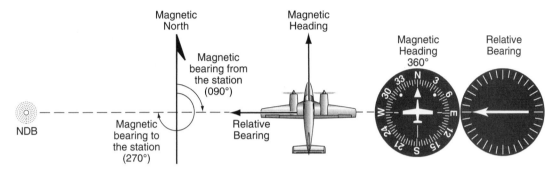

Figure 9-4 A magnetic heading of 360° and a relative bearing of 270°.

To summarize, heading + ADF = magnetic bearing to the station.

Better still, imagine the airplane is sitting on the tail of the ADF needle and the NDB is the center of the instruments. The tail of the needle shows the position of the airplane from the NDB.

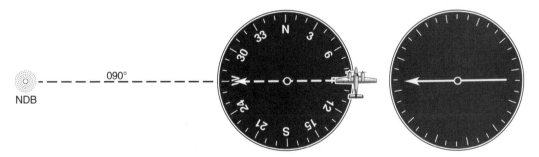

Figure 9-5 Imagined position.

Later, you will see reference to the bearing from the station as a *radial*. Strictly speaking, the term radial applies to the VOR but, in practical terms, both the VOR radial and the bearing from the NDB are used in the same way (remember the strict definition for examination purposes).

The concept of the radial and the imagining of the position of the airplane in relation to the aid as being on a particular radial are fundamental to all types of radio navigation that use pinpoint aids (rather than area navigation aids, such as GPS). For example, if you are on the 035 radial from Essendon, your bearing from Essendon is 035°M (035° radial) and the magnetic bearing to the station is 215°M.

To pinpoint the position of the airplane, we need to know the distance to the station or use position lines from two NDBs (by noting one and momentarily tuning to the frequency of the other). Some airplanes have two ADFs with two needles.

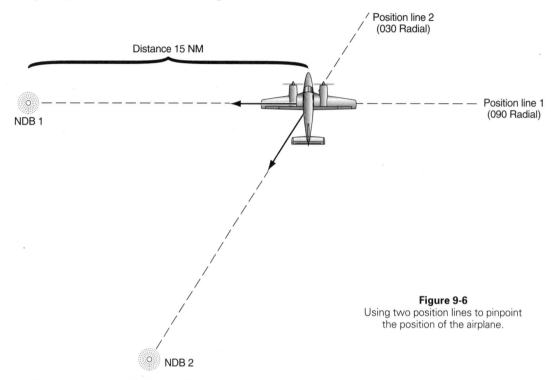

Figure 9-6
Using two position lines to pinpoint the position of the airplane.

Given that the ADF needle and the magnetic heading of the airplane are the two essential elements, you would expect these to be on one instrument. They are in modern airplanes (this instrument is then called a *radio magnetic indicator*, or RMI). It is much easier for the pilot to interpret them. In older airplanes, they are not only separate but the heading indicator must also be manually aligned to magnetic north (the magnetic compass could be used, but it is remotely positioned, less easy to read, and unstable in turns or in turbulence). More mental exercise is necessary with the older installations.

ADF and Heading Indicator Combination

To use the information from a particular NDB:
- the airplane must be within the operational range of the NDB;
- the ADF must be correctly tuned to the NDB frequency;
- the station must be identified (Morse code signal);
- the ADF needle must "come alive" in response to the signal, and it must settle in a direction that seems reasonable; and
- the HI must be aligned with the magnetic compass.

Intercepting a Track

Having become orientated with respect to an NDB, the pilot knows the answer to the question, "*Where am I?*" and now asks, "*Where do I want to go?*" and "*What heading do I steer to get there?*"

Visualizing Where You Are and Where You Want To Go

With HDG 070 and an RB of 100° left, you wish to intercept a magnetic track 270 *inbound* (to the NDB)—the 090 R. Visualize your position and the desired track.

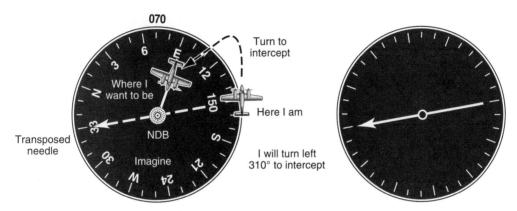

Figure 9-7 Visualizing an intercept on the HI.

With a model airplane on the tail of the needle tracking as desired, it becomes quite clear what turns are necessary to intercept the desired track. First, turn left to a suitable intercept heading, e.g. 360 for a 90° intercept of the 090 R while you think. Then turn to 310° for a 40° cut (intercept).

If you become disoriented, a simple procedure is to take up the heading of the desired track. Even though not on track, the airplane will at least be parallel to it, and the ADF needle will indicate which way to turn to intercept the desired track.

NDB/ADF Errors

A number of factors can act on the signals transmitted by an NDB and cause ADF indication errors and/or reduce the effective range of a ground station. During the hours of darkness and at distances far from the ground station, NDB signals are subject to significant interference by sky waves reflected from the ionosphere causing the ADF to have false indications, referred to as *night effect*. Rated coverage of NDBs at night may be reduced.

VOR

Principal advantages of the VOR over the NDB include:

- a reduced susceptibility to electrical and atmospheric interference (including thunderstorms); and
- the elimination of night effect, as VHF signals are line of sight and are not reflected by the ionosphere.

The reliability and accuracy of VOR signals allow the VOR to be used with confidence by day or by night in all weather conditions. It is used for:

- orientation and position fixing ("where am I?");
- tracking to or from a VOR ground station;
- holding; and
- instrument approaches.

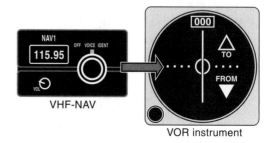

Figure 9-8 VOR equipment in the cockpit.

Many VORs are paired with a co-located *distance measuring equipment* (DME) ground station or TACAN (VOR-TAC). Selection of the VOR on the NAV/COM set in the cockpit also selects the frequency-paired DME or TACAN, thereby providing both tracking and distance information.

VOR Radials

A VOR station transmits signals in all directions. However, its most important feature is that the signal in any particular direction differs slightly from its neighbors. These individual directional signals can be thought of as tracks (or position lines) radiating out from a VOR ground station in much the same way as spokes radiate from the hub of a wheel.

There are 360 different tracks away from a VOR station, each separated by 1° and related to magnetic north. Each of these 360 tracks is called a *radial*. The 075 radial is actually a line bearing 075°M from the VOR station. *A radial is a magnetic bearing from a VOR.* The radials of a VOR are transmitted to an accuracy of ±2° or better.

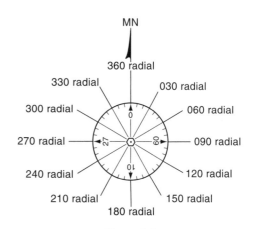

Figure 9-9
A radial is a magnetic bearing from the VOR.

Using the VOR

If an airplane is on the selected radial, the VOR needle—known as the *course deviation indicator* (CDI)—is centered (figure 9-10). If the airplane is not on the selected course, the CDI will not be centered.

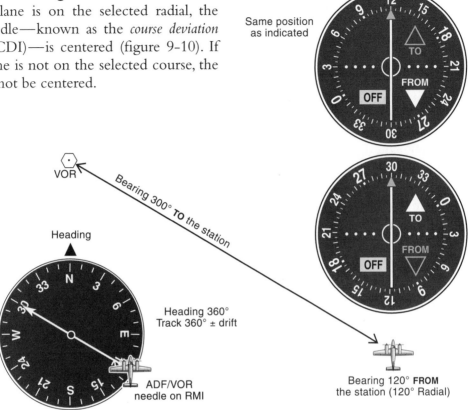

Figure 9-10 CDI centered.

The VOR indicator is not heading sensitive, which means that, regardless of the position of the airplane in relation to the selected course, the display will be the same on any heading. The case illustrated in figure 9-11 shows the same situation, except that a wind correction angle of 10° right is used by the pilot to counteract a wind from the right. The magnetic heading of the airplane is now 025 (rather than the previous 015).

Figure 9-11 Wind correction.

Preparing the VOR for Use

A NAVAID is of little value if the pilot does not use it correctly. Prior to using the VOR, a pilot must:

- ensure electrical power is available and switch the NAV/COM on;
- select the desired frequency—e.g. 113.2 MHz for the Brisbane (BN) VOR—as found on the applicable charts or in the A/FD;
- identify the VOR (*dah-dit-dit-dit, dah-dit,* which is the Morse code for BN—the coded identifier specified on the charts for Brisbane); and
- check that the *off* or *nav* flag is not showing—this indicates that usable signals are being received.

Orientation Using the VOR

Orientation is a term that refers to mentally picturing approximate position. The first step in orientation is to establish which radial the airplane is positioned on.

To find the radial, the pilot should:

- rotate the *omni-bearing selector* (OBS) until the CDI is centered; and
- note whether the *to* or *from* flag is showing.

For example, a pilot rotates the OBS until the CDI is centered—this occurs with 334 under the index and the *to* flag showing. Could another reading be obtained with the CDI centered?

In this case, the airplane is located on the 154 radial, and the CDI will be centered with either:

- 334 *to*; or
- 154 *from*.

The airplane may be heading or tracking in any direction.

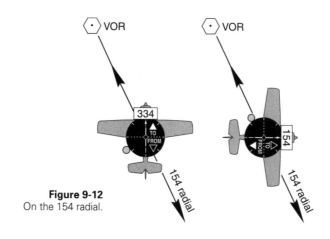

Figure 9-12
On the 154 radial.

Afterword

So, in a nutshell, that's what night flying is all about. We hope that we have motivated you to try flying at night. It is safe if approached with a professional attitude and with care. If you choose an experienced and motivated instructor and a well-equipped airplane, you will have many happy nights of flight.

My personal experience is flying over Australia and parts of South East Asia. But I would dearly love to fly my own aircraft over the Arizona desert at sunset or sunrise, over San Francisco Bay or the coast of Florida on a clear, dark night, or to fly high above the desert on a night when the stars are bright and there is little light from the ground.

I actually prefer to fly at night. It is smoother, there is less traffic, visibility is generally better, and other aircraft are easier to sight. Night flight is also accurate flight. In smooth conditions, you can fine-tune your instrument flying techniques and achieve accuracies that are more difficult to achieve during the day—and believe me, there is no more satisfying feeling than greasing the wheels onto the runway on a perfect night landing.

I hope you will enjoy your night flying as much as I have.

David Robson.

Index

B

balance 67, 69, 70
    effect of cupula on 72
    effect of middle ear on 68
    effect of otolithic organs on 70, 77
    effect of semicircular canals on 72, 73
    effect of vestibular apparatus on 70, 73
    false sensations of 69, 72, 76, 77, 78
    indications of in a turn 74–75, 76
balanced static system 12
bank attitude 6
barotitis 68
battery 14
beginning of daylight (BOD) 43
binocular vision 52
black-hole approach 63–64, 125
blackout 54
blind spot 52–53
boundary lights 89
bus bar 14

C

calibrated airspeed (CAS) 4
carbon monoxide 112
charts 84, 161
    as basis for mud map 166
    lighting information on 87
    and night visual navigation 117–118, 119
    reading at night 109
    weather charts 28
checkpoints 161, 162
civil twilight 81
    See also evening civil twilight, morning civil twilight, twilight
"CLEAROF" check 133
clock 10
    preflight inspection of 11
clouds 19
    abbreviations for 20
    classification system for 20
    danger of rising terrain under 47, 48
    distances from required for night VFR 86
    formation of 21, 22

clouds *continued*
    inadvertent flight into 132
    precipitation as indicator of 19
    types which promote icing 33–34
cockpit lighting 85, 109, 111
    failure of 144
    flashlight backup for 144
    recommended for night flight 84, 109, 111, 112, 114, 127
    red light 55, 84
    white light 84
cockpit organization 111
cold front 28–29
    dangers to aviation caused by 29
collision avoidance 84, 113
color blindness 54
color vision 51, 54
commercial pilots (night VFR) 82
compass correction card. See deviation card
compass instruments 3
    See also magnetic compass, remote indicating compass
configuration 100
control instruments 100
control-wheel steering (CWS) 17
coordination ball 7, 102
    preflight check of 11
course deviation indicator (CDI) 179
cruising levels
    reporting of 4
    selection of 164–165

D

dark adaptation 55, 112
datum 4
day 81
daylight 41
    beginning of 43
    duration of 43
    end of 43, 162
    perception of at altitude 44
dead reckoning (DR) 144
decision making 45–46, 48–49

radio magnetic indicator (RMI) 10, 176
radio navigation 173, 175
ram air pressure. See pitot pressure
rate-one turn. See standard-rate turn
recreational pilots (night VFR) 81
red light 55, 84
relative bearing 173, 174
remote indicating compass 9–10
    slaving of 9
rotary roll switch 17
route selection 162, 165
runway lights 90
    runway centerline lighting 89
    runway edge lights 89
    runway end identifier lights (REIL) 89
    threshold lights 89
    touchdown zone lighting 89

S

saturated adiabatic lapse rate (SALR) 30
seat of the pants 70
selective radial scan 98, 101, 130
servo 16
skid 7
skid ball. See coordination ball
slaving 9
slip 7
somatogravic illusion 7, 77
spatial disorientation 70, 77
spatial orientation 70
Special VFR (at night) 86
St. Elmo's fire 25
stable atmosphere 21
standard atmospheric conditions (ISA) 4
standard pressure 4
standard-rate turn 8, 99, 148, 150
stereopsis 52
student pilots (night VFR) 81
sunrise 41, 44
sunset 41, 44
supercooled water 31
supplemental oxygen 55

T

TACAN 178
takeoff
    common errors on 116
    day versus night takeoff 116
    engine failure on 141, 143
    at night 115–116
taxi light 113
taxiing
    at night 113–115
    progressive taxi 114
taxiway lighting 90, 114
terminator 43
thermals 21
thunderstorms 23, 24
    dangers to aviation caused by 26, 27
    diverting to avoid 26, 27
    flying through 28
    indicators of 26
    mature stage of 23
touch-and-go landing 127
traffic pattern. See pattern
transition altitude 4
transition level 4
true airspeed (TAS) 4
turbulence penetration 28
turbulence penetration speed (VB) 28
turn coordinator 3, 8
    use in autopilots 15
    use in partial-panel flight 148
    pretakeoff check of 11
turn indicator 3, 8
twilight 41
    duration of 42–43

U

unplanned night sectors 78, 107, 108, 132
unusual attitude 151
    causes of 151
    nose-high attitude 151, 154, 158
    nose-low attitude 152, 154, 156
    recognition of 151, 156
    recovery from 152, 154
    effecting spiral dive 152
urgency calls (pan-pan) 136, 137